COLLEGEPREPGENIUS
THE NO BRAINER WAY TO SAT* SUCCESS

Jean Burk

MoM
MAVEN OF MEMORY
PUBLISHING

Maven of Memory Publishing
Hurst, TX

Visit Maven of Memory on the Internet at

http://www.mavenofmemory.com.

Maven of Memory

Hurst, Texas

I dedicate this book to Christ,
for He is the Hope of Glory.

ACKNOWLEDGMENTS

I THANK MY HUSBAND, Jim, for his insistence on home educating our children and for the fact that he held down the fort all these years so I could stay home and raise and disciple our children. I am also grateful for his total support of my dreams as our business has grown.

I thank both Josh and Judah for not only being my guinea pigs through the years, but also for being the greatest blessings in my life. I also appreciate their keen insight and wisdom on this project and their desire to help make it the best on the market so other families could benefit from this information like they did.

I thank my dear friend Monica Brown for her entrepreneurial spirit that encouraged me to make my acquired research and knowledge available for others to glean from.

I thank Donna Boxerman for her incredible input on the math section.

TABLE OF CONTENTS

PART IV: THE WRITING SECTION

PART V: SCHOLARSHIP SEARCH

PART VI: Journal for Test Success

HOW TO USE THIS BOOK

BEFORE YOU BEGIN A program to improve your SAT or PSAT/ NMSQT score, you need to know your starting place. It's always a good idea to take a practice test in order to measure your strengths and weaknesses on the exam(s). To get a fair assessment, use the time constraints for each section. When taking a practice test, it is important to use materials from The College Board. They are the company that contracts with the ETS (Educational Testing Service), which writes the actual SAT and PSAT/NMSQT. Information on how to find real College Board material can be found on page 48-49.

Once you've established your starting position, you should thoroughly go through the College Prep Genius curriculum. Whether you are simply reading the textbook or using it with the College Prep Genius DVD curriculum, you should dedicate enough time to learn and understand all the strategies and information intended to help you better prepare for the SAT, PSAT/NMSQT and college itself. You may need to peruse this book two to three times to get a better understanding of the material.

As you learn the techniques and strategies for each section of the SAT, practice only on those sections in actual College Board materials (such as *The Official SAT Study Guide*). Start by practicing just one section at a time, then build up to two or three as you learn about different sections of the test. By the end of this program, you should be completing full tests. Always take practice exams in a similar testing environment as the actual test. If you use a page protector and wet erase pen or grease pencil, you can keep the practice tests clean for reuse or for multiple students.

This book is full of **ACRONYMS** to help you remember the tips and tricks of answering questions correctly. During your practice sessions, be sure to write the appropriate acronym at the top of the page to remind you of the recurring wrong answer patterns and traps that can be found on College

Start by practicing just one section at a time, then build up to two or three as you learn about different sections of the test.

Board tests. Take at least one test every week and spend the rest of the week correcting your mistakes. You can use the journal at the back of the book to help you keep track of your progress.

Learning lots of vocabulary words is not necessary for doing well on the test, but it can help you speak at a higher level and write better papers. You will need to learn the root words and negative and positive prefixes of the vocabulary words that are included in this text. It is **essential** to know and understand ALL the math definitions and how to apply them. Also, make sure you know the basic grammar concepts that have been supplied in the book.

Finally, take as many actual SAT practice tests as possible. When it is time to take the real test, you should be prepared and confident. Be sure to schedule more than one real test in a row, so that you will have multiple opportunities to do well.

TEST-TAKING TIMES

The SAT is offered 7 times a year: October- June and there are no penalties, for taking the test as many times as you want because colleges generally take the highest score. They often will take a composite score (Super Score) where they will take the highest score from different sections on different tests.

The PSAT/NMSQT can be taken three times but only counts for scholarships in the junior year.

BEFORE YOU BEGIN…

1. Establish a College Board account at www.collegeboard.com. On this site you can register for the SAT online. This will give you the opportunity to print your registration ticket for the test and view your scores and your essay after it has been graded. You will get access to testing times, deadlines and testing facilities and a database of colleges and universities. You can also get the "question of the day" for daily practice.

   It is best **not** to work the "question of the day" problem from the computer since the actual test will be on paper. (Print the screen or Turbo Snap® it.) You can then work the problem like the real test by using your pencil to circle, underline and mark through certain words. It is best to print these out and save them in a notebook so you can practice with them many times. (*Keep the paper clean by storing them in a page protector and using either a grease pencil or wet erase marker to work the problem.*) You can save the question of the day in an e-mail folder as a back-up as well as give you more test problems to practice with in the future since you will forget the questions.

2. Sign-up at www.fastweb.com, which will use your profile to send you scholarship offers and contests to enter.

3. Sign-up for "The No-Brainer Scholarship" Newsletter at www.collegeprepgenius.com. Enter your e-mail address in the Newsletter sign-up box at the upper right side of the page. You will receive scholarship contest information, success stories, college prep tips and more.

4. Take the My Motivation Test (Appendix C). Motivation is very important to help you keep on track. Discover what motivates you to succeed, and use it to help you set goals for preparing for the SAT and PSAT/NMSQT.

It is best not to work the problem from the computer since the actual test will be on paper.

Motivation is very important to help you keep on track.

PART I:

Introduction to the SAT

WHAT IS THE SAT?

THE SAT IS A test used to evaluate students for college entrance and scholarships. It is created by The College Board, and it comprises three sections: Critical Reading, Math and Writing. The maximum score on each of these sections is 800, with the highest possible score being 2400.

SAT is the SAT 1 Reasoning Test or better yet, a standardized assessment test. This is actually good to know because the test is written by a group of people who make sure each question follows the same pattern, standard, profile and criteria. That means that each test is designed to be inherently the same, with the same types of questions for each exam. Every question has been tested and tried out on students using previous tests. Therefore, you will never encounter a type of question on the SAT that hasn't already been tested by thousands of students on previous exams.

Why is the SAT standardized? Because students come from a variety of educational backgrounds and colleges needed a way to measure a student's math and language skills equally. Regardless of a student's academic background, the SAT is universal and puts everyone on an equal playing field. It doesn't matter where or when you take the test. The College Board tries to make sure each test is created with the same level of difficulty and integrity. Every exam is independently graded on the same equal curve, so that no test is more difficult than any other.

The fact that these tests are standardized should be a relief to you. The same basic concepts are tested in each test by changing up the same question over and over again. Every type of question recurs over and over again in each test. If a student can learn how to correctly answer a certain type of question, he or she can answer the same question correctly each time it shows up on the test!

The SAT is created by The College Board, and it comprises three sections: Critical Reading, Math and Writing.

All the standardized recurring test questions can be figured out through critical thinking.

This is a "reasoning" test, NOT a "content-based" or "subject matter" test. Reasoning can be defined as the use of reason to arrive at a conclusion. All the standardized recurring test questions can be figured out through critical thinking, which is the mental process for evaluating information with discerning logic. It gives colleges a fair assessment of the student's reasoning and analytical abilities needed for achievement in college. Therefore, to do well on this test you **do not** have to brush up on your classic literature or world history. Although students need a basic understanding of math and grammar, they do not need to have any specific knowledge about a certain topic. Students only need to learn how to answer the same basic questions that recur on every test.

By practicing and becoming very familiar with the patterns and question types, you can make finding the right answers automatic and easy. That's the purpose of this book: to help familiarize students with the recurring question types on the SAT and to give them the tools to practice correctly answering the question types until getting the right answer becomes second nature.

If you want to raise your SAT and PSAT/NMST score—learn how to correctly answer the recurring question types and PRACTICE…PRACTICE… PRACTICE!

When Should Students Start Preparing?

It's never too early to begin preparing for your future.

Immediately! Now is the time to start preparing for the SAT. It's never too early to begin preparing for your future. Waiting until you're a senior in high school is a HUGE MISTAKE! The more time you have to prepare, the more time you have to improve. Ninth grade is the ideal time to begin the SAT preparation process. Hopefully by starting early, you will be able to achieve your ideal score way before the deadlines of college and scholarship applications.

If, however, a student has waited to start preparing for this test somewhere in 11th or 12th grade, then he or she should make the SAT a priority and practice as much as possible at home before it's time to take the actual test. Then the student should schedule as many real tests as possible—especially seniors who only have a few opportunities left to take the test before graduation.

Learn to treat this test as a game. By learning to get in the mindset of The College Board (understanding how they write the questions and how they answer them), you can win at their game. Winning can mean higher test scores, entrance into the college of your choice, scholarships, etc.

Why Do Some Students Get Low Scores?

Many smart students do poorly on the SAT because they simply don't understand it. They approach it like a standard high school exam, trying to cram a bunch of information from school such as advanced vocabulary words and math formulas. Although knowing these things will be advantageous in life, it may be fruitless on the SAT.

The SAT is a reasoning test and not content-based. Every correct answer can be found without prior knowledge of the subject matter outside of knowing basic math and grammar. Instead of studying content, these students need to study how the tests themselves are set up and how the questions are written to determine how to answer them correctly.

Some students are naturally logically minded, and these types of tests come naturally. This doesn't mean that those who are not won't be able to do well on the SAT. It simply means that they will have to retrain themselves on how to look at these tests in a logical manner. Perfect practice makes perfect. In order for an athlete to excel at a particular sport, he or she will need to practice and train. The SAT is no different.

You do not have to be a left-brained to do well on the SAT math! You do not have to be right-brained to do well on the verbal sections! The SAT does not test how good you are at math or how good you are at language skills; it tests your ability to use critical thinking and reasoning using basic math and verbal concepts. Learning how to address the test with a logical perspective is the secret for any student to do well on this test! Remember, the questions are standardized, which means the same types of questions occur over and over again.

Understanding the logic behind the questions is the key to test success.

Understanding the logic behind the questions is the key to test success.

TEST OBJECTIVITY

The questions on the SAT are ALWAYS objective and NEVER subjective.

It is important to not be tempted to bring in your own opinion, read between the lines or look for any hidden agendas/ meanings.

The questions on the SAT are ALWAYS objective and NEVER subjective. This is good news because it means that no question is left up to personal opinion or interpretation. There is only <u>one</u> right answer and it can be found logically from the given information.

<u>Subjective</u>—One's own opinion; no concrete basis of definition; perceived

<u>Objective</u>—Factual without prejudices; truth can be derived from information

It is important to not be tempted to bring in your own opinion, read between the lines or look for any hidden agendas/meanings. Take every word literally. Students who understand this truth learn how to avoid subjective answer choices and correctly pick the right objective answers over and over again.

Don't justify why an answer should be right or wrong. There is no need to rationalize every answer choice; look for the obvious right one. If you are torn between two answer choices with similar meanings, they are probably both wrong since the test leaves no room for subjectivity. For example: A question asks you to define the meaning of a certain word, and the answer choices include happy, joyous and mirthful. You can be guaranteed that none of these three would be correct because they all have very similar meanings, which means if one of these is correct, you could argue the validity of the other two. This is what it means to be subjective.

There is only ONE correct answer for each question among the five multiple-choice answers. If a question appears to have more than one answer, you need to double-check your work. Remember, the test is <u>never</u> subjective. *(Important exception to note: Mathematical Student-Response questions may have more than one correct answer since there are no answer choices.)*

Keep your concentration on finding the wrong answers that follow The College Board patterns. If you find a problem in an answer choice, mark it off immediately and don't waste time. This helps you to not second-guess yourself or overthink the question. Make it your goal to quickly eliminate wrong answers as soon as you can.

TIME MANAGEMENT

More than anything, the SAT is a test of managing time. How fast and how well can you answer the questions in the allotted amount of time? Most students do NOT finish answering all the questions in each section. A failure of many students is approaching each question by trying to answer it in the conventional way, which usually takes much longer than the allotted time. In reality, The College Board designs most questions to be answered in 30 to 45 seconds or less. They write the questions with certain patterns in mind that point students to the answers quickly. There is usually a long way to work the problems, and then there is a shorter and more logical way to approach and attack each question type. It is the goal of this book to teach you how to approach problems the short way!

If you do not know how to answer a question, it is better to skip the question and go work the ones you do know. Often times our subconscious continues to work out problems in our head. If you get time, then you can come back and work the problem. Make sure you note that you skipped it with a star next to it. Don't spend a long and be determined to finish a question that you may or may not be able to work.

All questions are worth one point regardless of their difficulty level.

SAT STRUCTURE

The SAT is a three hour and 45 minute test (not including breaks) administered by ETS (Educational Testing Services). The format and structure of the test is standardized and it generally keeps the same patterns. The questions are not necessarily in order of difficulty. Students should look at each problem with a critical eye, regardless of where it is found in the section. The Critical Reading, Math and Writing sections are all divided into parts.

More than anything, the SAT is a test of managing time.

The SAT is a three hour and 45 minute test.

The Critical Reading section has two parts:

- Sentence Completion
- Passage-Based Reading
  1. Long Passage
  2. Short Passage
  3. Dual Passage

On the actual test, Critical Reading will be divided into three sections totaling 70 minutes in length: one 20 minute part and two 25 minute parts.

The Math section has two parts:

- Multiple Choice
- Student Response

Some of the types of problems will be Algebra 1 and 2, arithmetic and word problems, factoring and functions, geometry, measuring, number lines, statistics, probability and data analysis. There is no Trigonometry or Calculus.

On the actual test, Math will be divided into three sections totaling 70 minutes in length: two 25 minute parts and one 20 minute part.

The Writing section has four parts:

- Sentence Error
- Improving Sentences
- Improving Paragraphs
- Essay (topic will be provided at time of test)

There will be a total of 10 different parts of the actual SAT.

On the actual test, Writing will be divided into three sections totaling 60 minutes: one 10 minute grammar part, one 25 minute grammar part and one 25 minute essay.

There will be a total of 10 different parts of the actual SAT. Nine parts will come from the above three sections: Critical Reading, Math and Writing. The Equating section is part 10. This is an experimental section that is used to evaluate new questions and determine their difficulty level. This is based on the amount of wrong answers incurred. When your test is graded, the Equating section will not be counted toward your overall score. On the actual test, this section will be disguised as a part of the Critical Reading, Math or Writing section, and students will not be able to distinguish it from the rest of the test. Therefore, treat every section like it counts. However, the essay is never the experimental section.

SAT ANSWER SHEET

When you take the SAT, you will be given a test booklet (with all the questions) and an answer sheet with a bubble grid. The SAT answer sheet is separate from the test booklet. Only answers marked in the bubble grid will be counted. Once you've worked the problem, make sure to always bubble in the appropriate answers.

Because no one will grade your test booklet, the booklet is yours to work your problems in. Feel free to get messy. You will <u>not</u> get your SAT booklet back in the mail and no one will ever see it again. If you skip a question in the test booklet, put a star by it so when you bubble in your answers, you won't get off on the answering grid.

FUN TIP

Only bubble in your answers after you have worked the entire section. *Bubbling as you go wastes time!* However, be mindful of the time so you can make sure you mark your answers before the timer runs out. <u>Only bubbled-in answers will count regardless of how you answered in the test booklet.</u>

You <u>cannot</u> go back and forth between sections, return to earlier sections or spend more than the time allowed on any given section. You <u>may</u> move around a given section or just flip through it to see what's ahead.

The answer sheet is read and graded by a machine. Make sure your grid is bubbled in neatly and dark. If you skip a question, double-check to see if the darkened ovals line up with your test booklet.

SCORING THE SAT

The SAT has two scores: Raw Score and Scaled Score.

The Raw Score is determined by one point gained for every correct answer minus a quarter of a point subtracted for every incorrect answer. Skipped questions are not counted for or against your Raw Score. No points are subtracted for wrong answers in the Mathematical Student Response portion.

The Raw Score is converted to the Scaled Score (200–800) in each section using the equating process. This is a statistical evaluation that guarantees that each edition of the test is treated equally, so a score of 1800 on one test is equivalent to a score of 1800 on a different edition of the test.

In the Writing Section, the essay counts for approximately 30% of your Raw Score, and the multiple choice accounts for approximately 70% of your Raw Score. The essay is independently scored by two judges on a scale of 1 to 6, with the maximum score of a 12.

For more information about scoring, visit www.collegeboard.com/student/testing/SAT/scores/understanding/howscored.html.

The average SAT score is around 1500 out of 2400. The minimum score for college entrance varies from college to college.

The average SAT score is around 1500 out of 2400. The minimum score for college entrance varies from college to college. The starting score for scholarships is around 1800. Full scholarships can be obtained with scores around 2100. If a college does not consider the Writing section in their evaluation, then a score around 1400 (Math and Critical Reading) would be a good starting point for scholarships.

The fastest way to get your SAT results is to create an account at www.collegeboard.com. You can view your scores on the website around two weeks after the test date, and you can even view your essay, too.

If you would like a more detailed copy of the actual SAT you took, you can order The Question-and-Answer Service by The College Board for a small fee. You will receive a copy of a clean test booklet (not your original) and an answer sheet, a copy of your answers and the difficulty level of each question. However, this service is not available for every test.

Several factors can affect your score:

- How well you know and understand the test.
- The amount of test-taking strategies you know.
- How much practicing you have done.
- How adequately you prepared the day before the test.

SENDING SAT SCORES TO COLLEGES

When you sign up online for the SAT, you can request that your scores be sent to the colleges of your choice at no charge. You can send up to four free test scores to colleges. For a small fee, you can have your scores sent to additional colleges. For more information, visit http://www.collegeboard.com/student/testing/sat/scores.html. Some schools require Early Decision or Early Action, which means that scores are due by a certain deadline.

If you're worried about sending a bad test score to colleges, The College Board offers "Score Choice", which lets you choose to send only certain scores to select colleges. Sometimes a school wants to see ALL of your scores, but the good news is that most colleges only want to know a your highest score. They don't have time to go through every score. There is also <u>no</u> penalty for taking the test many times. Colleges don't average the scores, and many schools will take the highest scores from different sections on different tests to get you the best score. Therefore, it behooves you to take the test many times. The College Board will save SAT scores for up to two years.

CANCELING TEST SCORES

If after taking the test you feel like you really messed up, you can cancel your scores. There is a limited time frame that this can be done. A Test Cancellation form can be found at the testing facility, or you can contact The

When you sign up online for the SAT, you can request that your scores be sent to the colleges of your choice at no charge.

College Board. If you do cancel, your score report will be noted as "Absent or Scores Delayed."

THE SAT VS. OTHER TESTS

The ACT® (American College Test) is a content-based test and is also used for college entrance.

ACT

The ACT® (American College Test) is a content-based test and is also used for college entrance. It tests four areas: English, Math, Reading and Science. It also contains an optional Writing section. It includes some science reasoning and trigonometry, and it tests students' English grammar. The ACT is offered six times a year: September, October, December, February, April and June. Most colleges will take either the SAT or ACT, and if they prefer one over the other, they will usually convert the score.

SAT/ACT CONVERSION CHART

SAT (Prior to Writing Test Addition)	SAT (With Writing Test Addition)	ACT Composite Score
1600	2400	36
1560–1590	2340–2390	35
1520–1550	2280–2330	34
1480–1510	2220–2270	33
1440–1470	2160–2210	32
1400–1430	2100–2150	31
1360–1390	2040–2090	30
1320–1350	1980–2030	29
1280–1310	1920–1970	28
1240–1270	1860–1910	27
1200–1230	1800–1850	26

1160–1190	1740–1790	25
1120–1150	1680–1730	24
1080–1110	1620–1670	23
1040–1070	1560–1610	22
1000–1030	1500–1550	21
960–990	1440–1490	20
920–950	1380–1430	19
880–910	1320–1370	18
840–870	1260–1310	17
800–830	1200–1250	16
760–790	1140–1190	15
720–750	1080–1130	14
680–710	1020–1070	13
640–670	960–1010	12
600–630	900–950	11

NORMAL SCHOOL TESTS

When students approach the SAT like a normal test, they often don't receive the score they deserve. This is because the SAT is NOT like a normal school test. It is not an IQ test but a test of logic and critical thinking.

Normal School Test	SAT
No more than an hour long	Nearly four hours long
Harder questions receive more credit	All questions worth one point
Partial credit for correct parts	Only one right answer
Use long calculations for math (show work)	30 seconds or less for the math
Deeply examining passage content	Skimming passages
Essays that have been through several drafts	25 minute essay (unknown topic)
Rewriting correct grammar	Choosing from answer choices
Subjective answers	Objective answers

The SAT is NOT like a normal school test. It is not an IQ test but a test of logic and critical thinking.

SAT II

The SAT II is a subject-specific test that measures a student's mastery and knowledge in a specific subject area. You may have to take one or more of these tests if it is a requirement by the college of your choice. Certain colleges use them along with a student's transcript and SAT scores to help determine college preparedness. There are five categories of SAT II Subject Tests: English, Math, History, Science and Languages.

AP TESTS

AP (Advanced Placement) classes are college-level courses taken in high school. Students who complete AP courses are eligible to take AP exams designed by The College Board. These tests are scored on a scale of 1 to 5. A score between 3 and 5 may qualify a student for college credit at most colleges and universities.

CLEP TESTS

CLEP (College Level Examination Program) allows a student to earn college credit by taking qualified CLEP tests in a particular subject. The tests are designed to correspond to a one-semester class; they can sometimes cover up to a two-year course. The exams are generally 90 minutes long and cover specific information on knowledge and skills acquired about a certain subject. Be careful not to CLEP out of too many classes before starting college; it could cost you scholarships. It is usually better to do most CLEP tests after you are enrolled in college, but check with the school first. If you receive too many incoming hours, colleges may consider you a transfer student, disqualifying you for some scholarships.

FUN TIP

Strategies learned in this guide can also be used on other tests such as AP, CLEP, GRE, LSAT, ACCUPLACER...

WHAT IS THE PSAT/NMSQT?

PSAT/NMSQT STANDS FOR PRELIMINARY SAT/National Merit Scholarship Qualifying Test. Students in their freshman, sophomore and junior years of high school qualify to take this exam. Juniors who score in the top percentile can compete in the National Merit Scholarship Competition and/or The National Achievement Scholarship Program, which may qualify them for numerous scholarship opportunities that can include full tuition, room and board, graduate school money, study abroad stipends and more!

There are also 1,700 Special Scholarships that are awarded to high-scoring applicants who do not qualify to compete in the scholarship competitions, but who meet other specific criteria designated by scholarship sponsors. (businesses or corporations).

Registration for the PSAT/NMSQT must be done through a high school (not online). Parents should sign students up early to ensure a place, but you can sign up on the day of the test if there is room and they have enough booklets.

Both the SAT and PSAT/NMSQT are written by the ETS, which is a division of The College Board. Since both tests have the same creators, the question types are similar. They both contain three sections: Math, Critical Reading and Writing. However, the PSAT/NMSQT does not contain an essay and has up to Algebra 1 on the math section, whereas, the SAT contains some Algebra 2. The PSAT/NMSQT is only offered in October (third Wednesday or Saturday) and the SAT is offered seven times a year (October, November, December, January, March, May and June). The SAT is used for college entrance as well as scholarship opportunities, but the PSAT/NMSQT's sole purpose is to determine eligibility for the National Merit Scholarship program. Because the PSAT/NMSQT is basically a scholarship test, you'll want to make practicing for it a **priority**.

PSAT/NMSQT stands for Preliminary SAT/National Merit Scholarship Qualifying Test.

Because the PSAT/NMSQT is basically a scholarship test, you'll want to make practicing for it a priority.

Like the SAT, the PSAT/NMSQT is NOT a test of how much you really know. It is a test of reasoning skills and critical thinking.

There are benefits for taking the test early.

Both tests are important, and when you are studying test-taking techniques for one test, essentially you're also studying for the other test. Like the SAT, the PSAT/NMSQT is <u>NOT</u> a test of how much you really know. It is a test of reasoning skills and critical thinking. The key to doing well on the PSAT/NMSQT is to become familiar with the test patterns, learn test-taking strategies and then practice with College Board materials.

NATIONAL MERIT SELECTION PROCESS

Since 1971, the National Merit Scholarship Program has offered scholarships through the PSAT/NMSQT. Although the test is offered to freshmen, sophomores and juniors, only students who label themselves juniors on a test will qualify for the scholarship competition. The National Merit Corporation receives all the PSAT/NMSQT scores of juniors (approximately one million each year), and the competition begins.

Even though their scores will not count for the competition, students should take the PSAT/NMSQT for practice in both the freshman and sophomore years. There are two benefits for taking the test early. The first is the ability to gauge the scoring capability of a younger student and set realistic goals for future tests. The second is that students will receive their actual test booklet back in the mail, so they can go through it and pinpoint their strengths and weaknesses.

Test booklets will be sent back according to the school code on the test. Students need to make sure they correctly write their school code on the booklet, so it will be returned to the school. Homeschoolers will have a specific code for their state. Instead of going to the school, the test booklets and scores will be returned to the student's home address, and his or her score will not be calculated in the average of the testing facility. To find the home school code for each state go to http://www.collegeboard.com/student/testing/psat/reg/homeschool/state-codes.html.

The score that qualifies a student for the National Merit Scholarship Competition varies year to year and is dependent on where a student lives. The first step in the National Merit selection process is qualifying as a semifinalist. The Selection Index score is the determining factor in qualifying as a semifinalist. This score is the sum of all three scores from the Critical Reading, Math and Writing sections of the test. The index score must be in approximately the top 2% of the state to qualify; therefore, a student's score must be in the 97th to 99th percentile. Each state varies in its *cut-off* score (see chart). The best possible score is 240, or 80 points from each section. See chart on pg. 36

Although the test is in October, it's not until late August of the following year when The National Merit Corporation notifies the 16,000 students who have achieved Semifinalist standing. Around 50,000 students will be recognized (34,000 Commended Letters and 16,000 Merit Semifinalists). They will also send a list of the Semifinalists to four-year colleges and universities all over the United States. Local newspapers will get the same list to print the winners' names in their paper. Only students who opt to be added to the Student Search Service will be included in this list. This authorizes colleges to mail pertinent information to certain students they are interested in recruiting. The College Board does not report specific test scores. Students should check the box for the Student Search Service option on the PSAT/NMSQT exam <u>only</u> in their junior year. (This keeps unsolicited mail from coming in a student's freshman or sophomore year.) For many colleges, having students with National Merit recognition is a bragging right because semifinalists represent the top one percent of the nation. A semifinalist's mailbox will start filling up with college offers and information. Some of the perks that will be offered may include full tuition, room and board, study abroad stipends, graduate money, honors dorms, a computer, cash and more.

The next step in the process is the Finalist stage. To become a Finalist, the Semifinalists must complete the National Merit Scholarship application and mail it back on time. They must provide a high school transcript, show volunteer work, leadership skills and any awards received, letters of recommendation and a self-descriptive essay. (It is a good idea to get letters of recommendation from everyone that you work and volunteer for.) These letters play a big part when the scholarship committee reviews the applications.

Semifinalists must also take the SAT within a certain amount of time and earn scores that confirm the PSAT performance. Students should take the November and possibly the December SAT right after the October PSAT/

NMSQT since they should already be primed and practiced. Also, taking the October SAT right before the PSAT/NMSQT can help a junior prepare for their PSAT/NMSQT.

After students return their applications and the additional requested material, they should make a follow-up phone call to the National Merit Corporation to make sure they have received it. (847) 866-5100 (Add a delivery confirmation from the post office so you can have a record of your mailing and it can be easily verified.) Numerous students lose out on Finalist status and are terminated from the competition because they do not return all the information by the deadline.

In February, 15,000 out of 16,000 Semifinalists will advance to the Finalist standing. Each student will receive a Certificate of Merit, and out of those students, 7,900 Merit Scholars are chosen.

There are three types of Merit Scholarship awards: National Merit $2,500 scholarships, corporate-sponsored Merit Scholarships and college-sponsored Merit Scholarships.

There are three types of Merit Scholarship awards: National Merit $2,500 scholarships, corporate-sponsored Merit Scholarships and college-sponsored Merit Scholarships. All Finalists are considered for the National Merit $2,500 award, but only 2,500 will be awarded it. The 1,200 corporate-sponsored awards have certain criteria Finalists must meet to be considered. There are also 4,200 college-sponsored awards for Finalists who plan to attend certain institutions that offer this scholarship.

The $2,500 National Merit scholarships are chosen in late January by a committee of experienced college admissions officers and high school counselors. Finalists are evaluated on several criteria: transcript (course load and difficulty level, depth and breadth of subjects studied and grades earned); PSAT/NMSQT and SAT scores; the student's essay (his or her accomplishments, goals and interests); leadership abilities, community service and volunteer work; and letters of recommendation. The National Merit Corporation will notify students in March if they have been chosen for the National Merit Scholars program and the corporate-sponsored scholarship award. Those students chosen for the college-sponsored award will be notified from April through June.

NATIONAL ACHIEVEMENT AWARD

The NMSC (National Merit Scholarship Corporation) created the National Achievement Scholarship Program in 1964 to honor outstanding African American students. It runs simultaneously with the National Merit Scholarship program, and the two programs appear identical in structure, but the National Achievement Scholarship is operated and funded independently. African American students must request entry into the Achievement Scholarship program when they fill out Section 14 on the PSAT/NMSQT answer sheet.

Usually around 110,000 students enter the National Achievement Scholarship Program every year, and about 1,500 regional students achieve Semifinalist status. They will then compete for the next stage, and around 1,200 will advance to finalist standing. From these, Achievement Scholarship recipients are then selected.

The three types of NMSC awards are: National Achievement Scholarship ($2,500), corporate-sponsored Achievement Scholarships and college-sponsored Achievement Scholarships. Even though students can compete in both the National Merit Scholarships and the National Achievement Scholarships in the same year, they can only receive one monetary reward.

> **There are three types of NMSC awards: National Achievement Scholarship ($2,500), corporate-sponsored Achievement Scholarships and college-sponsored Achievement Scholarships.**

PSAT/NMSQT QUALIFYING SCORES

The qualifying score for the National Merit Competition varies yearly depending on what state you live in and the average test score the year you took the test. For example, qualifying scores for Texas have been around 216, but for Arkansas, they have been around 201. This helps to ensure geographic diversity of semifinalists. Out of a possible 240 points, in recent years, a test score anywhere in the 200–221 range has qualified students for the semifinalist status. There are also scholarship opportunities for those who score at the National Merit Commendable level (10–15 points below the semifinalist status).

Qualifying Scores for the Class of <u>2010</u> National Merit Semifinalists:

Alabama:	208	Montana:	204
Alaska:	211	Nebraska:	207
Arizona:	210	Nevada:	202
Arkansas:	203	New Hampshire:	213
California:	218	New Jersey:	221
Colorado:	215	New Mexico:	208
Connecticut:	218	New York:	218
Delaware:	219	North Carolina:	214
District of Columbia:	221	North Dakota:	202
Florida:	211	Ohio:	211
Georgia:	214	Oklahoma:	207
Hawaii:	214	Oregon:	213
Idaho:	209	Pennsylvania:	214
Illinois:	214	Rhode Island:	217
Indiana:	211	South Carolina:	211
Iowa:	209	South Dakota:	205
Kansas:	211	Tennessee:	213
Kentucky:	209	Texas:	216
Louisiana:	207	Utah:	206
Maine:	213	Vermont:	213
Maryland:	221	Virginia:	218
Massachusetts:	221	Washington:	217
Michigan:	209	West Virginia:	203
Minnesota:	215	Wisconsin:	207
Mississippi:	203	Wyoming:	201
Missouri:	211		

source: National Merit Scholarships
http://www.collegeplanningsimplified.com/NationalMerit.html

WHAT IS THE PSAT/NMSQT? 37

PSAT/NMSQT STRUCTURE

The Critical Reading section has two portions lasting 25 minutes each. These include:

- Long passages
- Short passages
- Sentence completion

The Math section has two portions lasting 25 minutes each. These include:

- Multiple choice
- Student response (10 questions)

The Writing section has one portion lasting 25 minutes. It includes:

- Identifying sentence errors
- Improving sentences
- Improving paragraphs

The total time given for the PSAT/NMSQT is 2 hours and 20 minutes.

GRADING

Each correct answer receives one point. Skipped questions do not count for or against the raw score. You lose 1/3 point for wrong answers with four answer choices and 1/4 point for wrong answers with five answer choices. NO points are subtracted for wrong answers in the student-response section. Then the raw scores are converted to the scaled score of 20–80. The best possible score from all three sections is 240. The average score for juniors who take the test is about 141.

If there is an asterisk by your Selection Index on your score sheet, it signifies that you did not meet the requirements for entry in the National Merit contest.

The total time given for the PSAT/NMSQT is 2 hours and 20 minutes.

Each correct answer receives one point. Skipped questions do not count for or against the raw score.

ALTERNATIVE TESTING METHOD

The student can take the SAT I in exchange for the PSAT/NMSQT, and the scaled SAT score will be converted to the scaled PSAT/ NMSQT score.

If a student misses (for any reason) his or her PSAT/NMSQT as a junior, there is still an opportunity to qualify for the National Merit program. Even though the PSAT/NMSQT is only administered once a year in October, a student has up to eight months (after the October PSAT/ NMSQT has been administered) to retake the test through the Alternative Testing Method. The student can take the SAT I in exchange for the PSAT/NMSQT, and the scaled SAT score will be converted to the scaled PSAT/NMSQT score.

This process begins with contacting the National Merit Corporation by calling (847) 866-5100 or sending a letter before the first of March stating that your student did not take the test and wants the extension/alternative testing time. You don't need to say why your student missed the test. The National Merit Corporation will send your student information showing future SAT test dates and tell him or her to use their code (code 0085) on the test. The scores will then go directly to The National Merit Scholarship Corporation. The National Merit Scholarship Corporation will take the highest score to apply for scholarship programs. Students will still be eligible for scholarships opportunities. These scores can also count for their SAT as well. Besides the National Merit code, students will need to put down the codes for the colleges they want to receive their SAT score. Students can take the SAT I every time it is offered that year for The National Merit Program.

The essay will not be counted!

Here are the steps to sign up for the Alternative Testing Method:

Letter Method

1. Write a letter to The National Merit Corporation (NMC) *(see example)
2. Print and FAX to NMC (847-866-5113)
3. Receive a packet in approximately 2 weeks

Online Method

http://www.nationalmerit.org/entering.php#miss

1. Fill out Score Recipient page (make sure you mark 11th grade)
2. Click "ADD"
3. Click "Search by Code"
4. In "School or Program Code" type in: 0085
5. Click "SEARCH"
6. Highlight "The National Merit Scholarship"
7. Click "ADD"

Make sure you do these steps every time you take the SAT in lieu of the PSAT/NMSQT. Students can have up to eight months to retake the test (November through June). The National Merit Corporation will KEEP THE HIGHEST SCORE!

Although this is a great alternative for juniors who missed their PSAT/NMSQT, it is best to take it if at all possible since it is a shorter an easier test than the SAT.

FUN TIP

Students must have their high school counselor sign-off on this or a parent if they homeschooled.

*Sample letter

Date:
To: The National Merit Corporation
Re: Info on Alternative Testing Entry into NMSC Programs

To Whom It May Concern:

I am a (parent, guardian, etc.) and my (son, daughter), who is a junior, was unable to take the PSAT/NMSQT in October. I understand that (he, she) is able to take the SAT 1 test in exchange for the PSAT/NMSQT.

Please send me all information concerning:

- Alternative testing entry into NMSC programs,
- SAT 1 testing dates and locations in (your city and county)

Student Contact information:
(Student's name)
Address
City, State, Zip

Thank you very much for your prompt response.

Sincerely,

Parent's name
E-mail
Phone

HOW TO PRACTICE?

THE KEY TO DOING just about anything well is to practice. Someone who plays a sport or learns an instrument can't expect to win a game or perform their best concert without practicing. The same applies with these standardized tests. After learning the test-taking strategies, you should practice with actual College Board practice tests.

It's a good idea to set a goal score for your tests, so you can know when you are achieving your goals. Make a daily/weekly schedule to practice as outlined below. It's also a good idea to study in groups or with other students who want to improve their SAT or PSAT/NMSQT scores, so you can encourage each other to excel. Setting solid, clear test goals, committing to total dedication and focusing solely on succeeding are essential to achieving high test scores.

The more you do this, the quicker you can find the recurring patterns and the faster you can answer the questions. The students who usually score the highest have made practicing a priority; they have put at least three to four hours a week into practicing over the entire year; and they have treated it like a marathon. Here is a basic <u>minimum</u> time *guideline for students for each year of high school:

- Freshman—one to two hours per week
- Sophomore—two to four hours per week
- Junior—four to six hours per week but more before the October PSAT/NMSQT
- Senior—six to 10 hours per week

*Your heaviest studying <u>should</u> be at least three months before the actual test you will be taking.

The key to doing just about anything well is to practice.

Put at least two hours a day during the week (studying and practicing) and 10 hours on the weekend. *(Remember, you are working toward a desired test score and/or amazing scholarships.)*

As you prepare, you will want to use College Board tests and materials exclusively for practice since they are the ones who make the SAT and PSAT/NMSQT. When not practicing with full-length tests, work in the sections separately (i.e. Critical Reading only). Work the precise amount of problems with the correct time restrictions.

It goes without saying that most students who make these tests a priority will usually spend less time on the computer and watching TV and more time studying and reading than other students. This doesn't necessarily mean that they can't be social or have a job, but it means they probably won't put as much time into those areas as other students.

You need to tackle test preparation with a clearly defined strategy.

PRACTICING STRATEGY

You need to tackle test preparation with a clearly defined strategy. You must first master test-taking techniques, learn to answer the questions quickly and correctly and then finish the test on time. The best way to help lessen test anxiety is to gradually expose yourself to the real test environment; this will help to condition you for this mental marathon on test day. Your level of success depends primarily on your preparedness. Here's a workable practice strategy.

1. Go through each section (Critical Reading, Math and Writing) of *College Prep Genius* one at a time.
    a. Learn all about the hidden strategies and recurring patterns.
    b. Memorize the acronyms for each section
2. Set aside adequate time to practice sections from the real test.
    a. Use only College Board material.
    b. Keep notes open while working the problems.
3. Keep records of missed questions in "The Journal for Test Success."
    a. Go back over them and rework them.
    b. Review them to make sure you have conquered that pattern.

4. Take a full-length practice test with no time constraints.
5. When you have become familiar with each section, start timing the tests like the real test. Time each section correctly!

Learning strategies is important but you must know basic concepts or the shortcuts won't help much. Anxiety on the math section is often just a fear of the unknown. To overcome this, make learning math (terms and strategies) a priority. The SAT math generally consists of simple concepts that are not difficult to master. Identify your weaknesses but don't forget to work on your strengths. Concentrate on one section at a time and practice in long blocks to build up stamina.

LEARNING STRATEGIES

This book is full of strategies and techniques to answering questions correctly on the SAT. Most of the tips are put together in ACRONYM form, so you can remember them easily. A good idea is to use index cards to help you memorize the acronyms. At the top, write horizontally the section. Along the left side, write the ACRONYM vertically and big. Next to each letter, write the long version.

On the flipside, do the same but write the shorter version. In the beginning, refer to the longer side as you are learning the ACRONYM. Then switch to the shorter version. After you have memorized each ACRONYM, start writing the word(s) at the top of the appropriate page. (There is a section on the teaching DVD that contains the ACRONYMS for easy memorizing.)

THE PENCIL IS VERY IMPORTANT

Your pencil is your best tool on taking the SAT and PSAT/NMSQT. Writing in your test booklet is not only acceptable but is preferable in getting high scores. You will use it to write acronyms, note the time each section starts, underline words, circle sentences, rewrite math equations, redraw math diagrams, draw arrows and mark out wrong answers. You will also use it to star questions that you skip so you don't forget to come back and work them.

The SAT math generally consists of simple concepts that are not difficult to master.

Very importantly, use your pencil to circle the correct answer that you've arrived at. This will make it easier to transfer the correct answer onto the answer sheet.

Keep your pencil moving at all times and don't lay it down during the test. Our minds are limited to a few thoughts at a time so ALWAYS write important information down in the test booklet. This frees up a clouded mind and allows you to freely move from one question to another. To minimize mistakes, NEVER work problems in your head.

MARKING THE CORRECT ANSWER

> Once you've learned the strategies and shortcuts for answering test questions, it's simply applying the logical reasoning you've learned to real test questions.

Once you've learned the strategies and shortcuts for answering test questions, it's simply applying the logical reasoning you've learned to real test questions. Here's an acronym for answering questions correctly:

R ead all the answer choices
E liminate obvious wrong ones first
A dd each answer choice into the question
D etermine the right answer and mark it confidently

If you get "stuck" on a question, reread it and break it down. (Often times your first impression is correct.) Write down key elements from the question, eliminate obvious wrong answers and make sure your selected answer choice actually answers the question. Never change an answer UNLESS you are certain it is wrong.

GUESSING ON THE TEST

The College Board writes questions so that most students will read and gloss over the key word(s). This usually causes them to fall for wrong answer choices that "look" correct but are actually wrong. Because students don't know how to answer the question properly, they make "educated" guesses. The problem with doing this is that if you get the question wrong, guessing will cost you points from your raw score. It is usually better to skip the question than to get it wrong by guessing. Guessing when you don't understand the logic behind the question or how it is set up can lead to a lot of points subtracted from your raw score.

There is only one right answer and The College Board usually leaves a way for you to figure it out as long as you can recognize the recurring patterns on the test. If you don't know the answer, it is generally better to leave the problem blank. *Make sure you put a mark next to the skipped questions as well as a mark on the grid-in so you won't get off on your grid-in answer sheet.*

SKIPPING QUESTIONS

Don't waste time on a question that you are "clueless" about. Move on to answer the ones you do know. Your subconscious may work it out in your head and if you get time, you can come back and answer it. All questions are worth one point each. (You do not get more points for difficult questions.) Make sure you note the ones that are skipped so you can attempt them later and/or appropriately skip them on the answer sheet. You can skip about one-twelfth of the questions and still receive a score of 700; skipping a fourth of the questions can yield a score of 600; skipping a third of the questions can still achieve a score of 500.

You could actually skip a few questions in each section (Critical Reading, Math and Writing) and still achieve a perfect score if all of your other answers are correct. All questions are worth one point, so an occasional skip should be okay.

PACE YOURSELF

Don't rush to finish the test early. Carefully read each question with a very critical eye and work it quickly but accurately. Double-checking answers should be done at the end of each section to make sure you have enough time to finish the test.

There is only one right answer and The College Board usually leaves a way for you to figure it out as long as you can recognize the recurring patterns on the test.

You could actually skip a few questions in each section (Critical Reading, Math and Writing) and still achieve a perfect score if all of your other answers are correct.

> **When you go back over your practice tests, it's a good idea to identify the types of errors that you are making.**

GRADING PRACTICE TESTS

When you go back over your practice tests, it's a good idea to identify the types of errors that you are making. This can help you pinpoint your problem areas so you can work on them.

The ABCs of Errors:

> **A**: Asinine ☹ (Made a careless, dumb mistake)
> You didn't double-check your work
> You didn't circle what it was asking or you misread the question

> **B**-Blank ◯ (Drew a blank because you forgot how to work it)
> Memorize ACRONYMS to help you remember steps to success
> PRACTICE daily/weekly to keep you fresh on techniques

> **C**-Clueless **?** (Didn't know how to work this problem)
> Skip it (All questions are worth one point, so move on)
> Commit to learning how to work it
> Write the problem down in your journal and review it periodically

When you go over your practice questions, write an A, B or C next to your wrong answers. Analyze what type of errors you keep making over and over again. Make a plan to work on them until they are drastically reduced and hopefully eliminated altogether.

KEEPING A JOURNAL

It's important to keep a record of your missed questions (in the "Journal for Success" in the back of this book) because this will allow you to conquer them. From doing your first practice test (without strategies) to learning short-cuts, taking the "Master the SAT Class," to practicing with College Board material, you can learn to figure out your strongest and weakest parts of the test.

Analyze each practice test by keeping a journal of which questions you get wrong. On this list, make a note of the question and the date. Return to it in a week and then in a month. If you can now remember what you did wrong and how to correct it, you can remove it from your list.

If not, keep revisiting it until you fully understand the question, its pattern and how to solve it. (For extra help, you could copy the entire wrong questions in your journal and review them before going to bed.) This can help solidify them in your head and when you are faced with similar problems on the real test, it'll be old hat to you.

By spending more time on your weak areas, you can start to see more improvements.

Take the practice tests over and over again (since you'll forget the questions) and then check your journal to see if you conquered the questions you got wrong on a previous practice session.

It is important that you understand basic rules of math and grammar before learning strategies. If these areas are hindering your score, conquer them first. This can be done by reviewing the basics until you understand them. If this isn't working, you may want to seek one on one help in a particular area. After this, your goal is to streamline your energy into working on your weak points of the test.

Don't forget about working on your strong points, either. This keeps you fresh and will help boost confidence on your test-taking skills.

RIGHT FRAME OF MIND

As you practice, it is important to keep a few tips in mind:

- Don't fixate on your score.
- Focus on familiarizing yourself with the test-taking strategies.
- Look for recurring patterns on how to answer questions quicker.
- Make a game plan of what time of day/week you will study.

By spending more time on your weak areas, you can start to see more improvements.

- Pace yourself with your own watch.
- Get a study partner—someone to keep you accountable.
- Set a test score goal and then work to achieve it.
- Be prepared to put a lot of time in—success is not instant.

ACTUAL PRACTICE SAT TESTS

When you practice taking the SAT, you should only use actual tests that were created by The College Board and The Educational Testing Service (ETS).

When you practice taking the SAT, you should only use <u>actual</u> tests that were created by The College Board and The Educational Testing Service (ETS).

The *Official SAT Study Guide* 1st Edition has eight <u>actual</u> SATs to practice with and the 2nd Edition has 10 (only three are different). The *10 Real SATs* has 10 old tests that can still be practiced with (however, do not work the eliminated sections: analogies and quantitative comparisons).

Here is a list of College Board tests and materials. Most of which you can acquire from www.collegeboard.com:

1. *The Official SAT Study Guide* by The College Board 1st or 2nd Edition

2. *The Official SAT Online Course

3. T*aking the SAT Reasoning Test* booklet
    (available free at most high schools in the guidance counselor's office)

4. *One on One with the SAT (a CD sent in the mail)
    *SAT Prep Packs (downloads off the site)
    Free SAT test (download)
    SAT question of the day
    Free mini-test

5. *The 10 Real SATs* by The College Board
    (First, second and third editions are available.)
    Each edition contains some different tests—just omit eliminated sections.

*Some students find it very difficult to answer these questions on the computer since there is no paperwork. To make it easier, some students have used a program that captures the picture on the computer screen, copied it to a word processor and then printed it. Working questions on hard copy is more like taking the **real** test. (Save them in a folder so you can rework them later.)

ACTUAL PSAT/NMSQT TESTS

As of March 2005, the main difference between the PSAT/NMSQT and SAT test is that there is no essay or Algebra 2 on the PSAT/NMSQT. To practice for the PSAT/NMSQT, you can still use the <u>same</u> SAT materials. You will want to cover Math, Critical Reading/Verbal and Writing. Some other PSAT/NMSQT resources are:

1. *"Taking the PSAT/NMSQT"* booklet
   (available free at most high schools in the guidance counselor's office)

2. Retired actual PSAT/NMSQT tests (unavailable at this time)
   (http://store.collegeboard.com/enter.do; click on PSAT/NMSQT)

3. College Board, *The Real SAT II Subject Tests*
   ISBN 0-87447-7034 (has Writing Section)

4. College Board, *The Real SAT II Subject Tests*
   ISBN-0-874476771 (has Writing Section)

5. College Board, *The Real SAT II Subject Test*
   ISBN 0-874475-99-6 (out of print)

6. PSAT/NMSQT Test Booklets
   (returned after the student takes the actual test)

   Every year pick up a new free SAT and PSAT/NMSQT test booklet from the guidance counselor; they can be reused as well.

To practice for the PSAT/ NMSQT, you can still use the same SAT materials.

ADDITIONAL STUDY MATERIALS

LOGIC CURRICULUM

It would certainly behoove you to work some logic curriculum to help prepare you for the SAT and PSAT/NMSQT. These tests require you to THINK, and practicing with logic materials can aid in this area. Use material or games that can stimulate your creative thinking. Crossword puzzles and brain teasers could also be a plus. Treat the test as a challenging puzzle that can be figured out logically. The material on the test is somewhat limited but the deliberation behind the problems is very definitive.

CLASSIC LITERATURE

When preparing for the Critical Reading section of the SAT and PSAT/NMSQT, reading classic literature can help build and enhance a student's vocabulary. There are so many good books to choose from! When looking for a book to read, choose one that is well-known, enlarges your knowledge, has lasting value, has withstood time, has a high standard and is unabridged. (Type "classic books" in a search engine for starters.)

SAT VOCABULARY WORDS

Learning a lot of vocabulary words is not necessarily the key to scoring higher on the Critical Reading Section. The College Board is the only one who knows what words will be on the test. You could learn 4,000 vocabulary words and not one of them might be on the test. Since the SAT is a logic test, there are ways to figure out the words without knowing them. However, having a good grasp of vocabulary will help you communicate more effectively and intelligently. A few of the words you learn may even end up on the SAT or PSAT/NMSQT. Learning difficult vocabulary words that may be on the SAT can be painlessly mastered in a fun way by the new VocabCafe Book Series. Check these out at www.vocabcafe.com.

TAKING THE REAL TEST

THE SAT IS OFFERED seven times a year, starting in October and ending in June. You can take the SAT as many times as you want. All your scores will be recorded, however, prospective colleges usually only consider your top scores. If you have any doubts, contact the admissions office at the college of your choice.

There are **no penalties** for taking the SAT many times. Most colleges just drop the lowest scores (they don't average them.) Many colleges will take the highest scores from each section from different tests. Most colleges don't have cut-off dates to receive SAT scores, but you should always check with the college of your choice.

Tests are held on Saturday mornings. If you can't take a Saturday test due to religious obligations, you can take it on a Sunday. You will need a signed letter from your clergyperson written on official letterhead to qualify. You will use the code 01000 when taking the test; all future tests will be administered on a Sunday.

Parents or students can sign-up by mail or on the official web site, www. collegeboard.com. Please sign up early because deadlines and late fees may apply. There is a fee to sign up for the test, but waivers are available for individuals that may find this fee a financial burden. You can receive up to four free SAT tests in your junior and senior year. Check with the high school's guidance counselor for the criteria.

The PSAT/NMSQT can only be registered for at your local high school up until the day of the test if there is room. There is a nominal fee to take it but waivers are available at local guidance counselor offices.

There are no penalties for taking the SAT many times.

CHOOSING A TEST LOCATION

It is very important to know the reputation of the school/test site before deciding where to take your test. There are horror stories of proctors that have cut the test-taking time short or forgot to set the timer altogether!

There are other stories of proctors who have totally humiliated outside students by standing over them or isolating them in the hallway. Make sure to talk to others about their personal experience at the local schools where they took their tests. *You do not have to take the test at the school you attend, and homeschoolers should be able to take it at any scheduled testing facility.*

Practice Right Before The Real Test

It is best to prepare well for your first actual test because this will help boost your confidence.

It is best to prepare well for your first actual test because this will help boost your confidence. If you are not happy with your score, don't get discouraged, but refine your study plan. Besides using ONLY practice tests from The College Board, you should also practice the same way that the real test is given. This means you should take the test in its entirety with only a five-minute break between sections.

You should also take it at the same time as the real test (this is usually around 9:00 in the morning). Always use the same watch and calculator in practice that you plan to use during the real test. To save time and frustration, be familiar with the rules for each section before taking the real test. Don't waste time reading the rules at the real test. They don't change, so know them ahead of time.

Read some of your old essays before the real test just to refresh you. As you will see in the essay section, old essays will come in handy for the real test. The essay is usually the first section of the SAT when you open up the booklet to take the test.

The DAY Before the Test

Do not do any SAT work the day before the actual test. Relax and go to bed ON TIME. Make sure you have the correct driving directions, gas in the tank and all your supplies ready. Know the time you should arrive on test day (the time will be on your ticket).

The Morning of the Test

- Wake up with enough time that you will not be rushed. You do not need any added pressure.
- Eat a light breakfast.
- Leave early.

What to Bring

Bring three to four #2 sharpened pencils with good erasers. Mechanical pencils are banned! Also bring a manual pencil sharpener; this can keep you out of the long pencil sharpener line if all your pencils break. Highlighters are also banned from the test. It is a good idea not to use them on your practice tests since you want to work them like the real test.

It is always good to use the same calculator that you have been practicing with at home. Always bring one to the test just in case, and make sure it has fresh batteries. Simple functions are all that are needed, so don't waste your money on expensive calculators. One with exponents and square roots are allowed. (You are only allowed to use it during the math sections, and sharing one will be cause for dismissal from the test.)

Acceptable calculators include graphing calculators, scientific calculators and four-function calculators (although this option is not recommended). BE WARNED—students may be seated away from other students (at the test proctor's discretion) if their calculator has characters that are one inch or bigger or if it has a raised display where others may see it. (If needed, students should bring one that has exponents and square roots on it.)

Do not do any SAT work the day before the actual test.

It is always good to use the same calculator that you have been practicing with at home.

Unacceptable calculators include laptops and portable/handheld computers; any calculator that has a (typewriter-like) keypad, uses an electrical outlet, makes noise or has a paper tape; electronic writing pad or pen-input/stylus-driven devices; pocket organizers; and cell phone calculators.

Bring a watch with either a second hand or a chronometer. Please try to use this same watch when you're practicing for the SAT. You cannot bring any timers with alarms.

Dress in layers or bring a sweater. Schools like to keep the rooms cold since there are usually a lot of people taking the test. Dress comfortably.

Food is normally not allowed, but you may be able to bring snacks to eat during the breaks. If you bring a water bottle, it cannot have a label.

No cell phones or backpacks are allowed in the test.

If you are easily distracted, you may want to bring earplugs.

You will need your picture I.D.* and the ticket you got when registering for the test (can be printed off The College Board website).

*Students who do not have a driver's license or who are homeschooled and do not have a school I.D. can get a State issued ID for non-drivers, which costs around $15. It takes 2 to 3 weeks to process from your state's Department of Public Safety or Motor Vehicles. Homeschoolers can also get an ID form from their public school, with the school's letterhead, and then attach a passport photo. For more information, visit http://www.collegeboard.com/student/testing/sat/testday/id.html.

AT THE TEST

Stay calm and trust in the fact that you have been preparing for this day. Take deep slow breaths to help clear your mind if you feel anxious. Treat it as a game that can be beat. Relax! Do your best. Remember, you can always take the test again.

You will want to pace yourself just like you've done during your practice tests. Use the same watch during all tests. If the watch has a count-up timer, start it at the beginning before each test and occasionally glance at it to see how much time you have left. If you are using a second-hand watch, set both hands at <u>twelve o'clock</u> before each section of the test (start the watch when the proctor starts the test). Depending on the length of the test, you can keep an eye on how much time you have left.

Watch the time. Don't rely on the proctor to give you a warning. Use your own chronometer watch or set your second-hand watch at 12:00 for each section. (*This keeps you from having to calculate how much time is left*.) Use your breaks to recharge your thinking. Concentrate on the test; don't waste time on thinking about the score results.

Watch the time. Don't rely on the proctor to give you a warning.

If at first glance, the question seems to be "B" (draw a blank) or "C" (clueless), then skip it and move on. Put a star by it and come back to it if you have time. Remember, every question is worth one point so there is no need to waste time on questions that you know you can't answer.

Always double-check your work. This only takes a few seconds but could save you points.

Don't ever change an answer unless you know for certain it is wrong!

Always double-check your work. This only takes a few seconds but could save you points.

EVALUATING YOUR PERFORMANCE

If you would like to thoroughly evaluate your test results, the Question-and-Answer Service is available for three SAT tests (October, January and May). If you take any of these three tests, you will have up to five months to purchase the service for a fee.

They will receive in the mail:
- A clean copy of the test booklet
- A record of their answers and the correct answers
- Information on question difficulty levels

Having this test booklet will also allow you to use it again for practice.

A FAIR TEST FOR EVERYONE

The College Board strives to make sure the SAT and PSAT/NMSQT are unbiased and offer a fair testing experience for everyone who takes them. The SAT is available for all high school students, regardless of race, religion or economic standing. If you can't afford the test, fee waivers (up to four) are available for juniors and seniors at most local high schools. You will need to contact a local guidance counselor for more information. You will give you a form with a waiver number. You will need to find out your correct code by calling (212) 713-8000 or (609) 771-7600. Then go to www. collegeboard.com, register and add those codes to the form. Some PSAT/NMSQT waivers are available through the coordinators at most local high schools. (Apply early!) Qualifying students can receive up to 4 waivers in the last two years of high school: SAT II test waivers can be used in ninth through twelfth grade. These students may also have their college application fees waived. Waivers CANNOT be used for late registrations.

GRADING MISTAKES

If you think your test has been unfairly graded, you can request that your test be hand scored for a small fee. Call (609) 771-7600 for more information.

UNFAIR TESTING ENVIRONMENT

Sometimes, there can be major distractions that may hinder your success on the test. If this occurs, you can complain and possibly get a new test or other compensation. Make sure that others do this as well; this adds credibility when The College Board is aware of other complaints.

Contact: Fair Test
phone: (617) 864-4810
fax: (617) 497-2224
www.fairtest.org

If you think your test has been unfairly graded, you can request that your test be hand scored for a small fee.

DYSLEXIA, DISABILITIES AND SPECIAL NEEDS

Accommodations can be made for students with special needs, and time constraints can be lessened. However, going through the process of obtaining special accommodations could take many months. Parents will need to schedule a battery of tests, obtain the diagnostician's report for their student, arrange for and implement accommodations at school and have these accommodations in use in the school setting for a minimum of four months (a College Board rule). When applying for special accommodations please keep in mind the time it takes for The College Board to process and grant or deny the request. Families may be limited to working with the school's calendar/timetable for testing (ARD meetings and creating IEPs). Ideally, the process of preparing for standardized tests should start in the student's freshman or sophomore year, to allow time for The College Board accommodations to be in place before the PSAT/NMSQT in the student's junior year. For more information about forms, eligibility and documentation, visit http://www.collegeboard.com/ssd/prof/physical-disabilities.html.

The 504 plan specifies that no one with a disability can be excluded in federally funded programming, and that all should be given the opportunity to perform at a level equal to their peers. In this case, disability could include physical impairments, injury, disease or chronic conditions.

When applying for special accommodations please keep in mind the time it takes for The College Board to process and grant or deny the request.

ADULTS AND THE SAT

Adults can take the SAT if desired. However, many colleges do not require it for older applicants. Please check with the school of your choice. There is no age limit on taking the SAT even if a student has graduated from high school.

HOMESCHOOLERS

For the homeschooler, many colleges weigh SAT scores heavily because they are an unbiased evaluation of academic prowess. So, homeschooled students should make this test a priority. Homeschoolers are at no disadvantage when taking the SAT. The material on the SAT is not an exclusive curriculum found only at public or private schools. The test is a "reasoning" or logic test, and the key to doing well is to learn the hidden strategies and recurring patterns that are usually found on these tests.

PSAT/NMSQT Test scores will automatically be sent to the high school code placed in the grid on the test. To ensure that scores are sent to your home, use the appropriate home school code for your state in the blank provided. Tests with the home school code will not affect the average scores of the testing facility. The home school code for your state can be found at: http://www.collegeboard.com/student/testing/psat/reg/homeschool/state-codes.html.

PLAN FOR TEST SUCCESS

1. Read the book *College Prep Genius*.
   Make sure to learn all the good information about test strategies, the college interview process and how to get scholarships. Take the "Master the SAT Class" in person or via the DVD curriculum.

2. Learn the ACRONYMS for each section.
   After you memorize these, you can write them in your test booklets to help you remember what to do in each section. (*Notes are NOT allowed at the test, but you can write* all over *your booklet*.)

3. Practice with College Board tests.
   They can be found in bookstores, guidance counselors' offices and at www.collegeboard.com. If you start preparing as a freshman, you should spend at least one to two hours per week practicing. Sophomores starting out should spend two to four hours, and juniors new to the test need to spend four to six hours per week taking practice SATs. If you've waited until you're a senior, it's a good idea to spend at least six to 10 hours a week preparing. Your heaviest studying should begin at least three months before the actual test.

4. Know the rules for each section ahead of time.

   The rules for each section of these tests always stay the same, so learn them long before you take the real SAT and PSAT/NMSQT. This not only saves time, but you will already know what to expect in each section.

5. Create a similar test environment.

   Many students don't realize that these tests are very long and require mental endurance to finish them without running out of steam. The SAT itself is over 3½ hours long. One way to prepare for this academic marathon is to practice just like the real test. Creating a test environment like the real test can eliminate any surprises and help with test success. Practice like this:

   a. Start the practice test around 9:00 a.m.
   b. Take only a five-minute break in between sections.
   c. Use the same watch and calculator that you will use at the real test.
   d. Make sure the testing area is free of distractions.
   e. Time each section correctly.
   f. Use a watch with a chronometer or set a second-hand watch at 12:00 for each section.
   g. Keep several sharpened pencils nearby.

6. Take PSAT/NMSQT for practice in both freshman and sophomore years.

   The score won't count, but it will help familiarize you with the test, and you'll also get your test booklet back in the mail. It usually arrives in the spring after the October test. The test score arrives later. When you receive it, go over your mistakes and find the patterns of the questions you missed. You can also use the booklet to retake the test later and see how much you have improved. (*Retaking it can be beneficial since most students forget the questions.*)

7. Take the PSAT/NMSQT in your junior year when it counts.

   This test will not only measure how well you might do on the SAT, but it's also an opportunity for amazing scholarship offers from colleges all over the nation.

Students who score in the semifinalist range can literally get a full-ride to numerous colleges because they are in the top 1% of the nation. This test only counts in their junior year or the third year they take it.

8. Take several SAT tests in a row, and take it many times.
Take two to three tests in a row, since you will already be studied up. There are no penalties for taking the SAT many times, so you should take it until you get your desired score. Colleges do not average the tests but take the highest scores. Many colleges will even take the highest score from each section from different tests to get the student's best overall score. Every college is different when it comes to their desired entrance score as well as entry level for starting scholarships, so make sure you check with the college(s) of your choice.

9. Record your scores in your "Journal for Test Success."
This will help you track your progress.

PART II:

THE CRITICAL READING SECTION

CRITICAL READING SECTION

Most students cringe at the thought of the Critical Reading section on the SAT and PSAT/NMSQT. Having to read four passages and answer 24 questions in 25 minutes is frightening! Yes, that's about a minute a question, not counting the time it takes to read the passages. It's practically impossible to finish this section on time if you try to tackle it the normal way.

On school exams, students are taught to read all the questions first, then the passage and then all the questions again. Naturally, this is the same approach that most students take when it comes to standardized tests like the SAT and PSAT/NMSQT. Of course when they do this, they run out of time. This results in a lot of blank answers and an unsatisfactory score.

On top of the incredible time constraints, students are dumbfounded by questions that seem to have more than one correct answer. It seems like not only do students need a supernatural speed-reading ability, but also psychic powers! Fortunately, many mortal students have aced both the SAT and PSAT/NMSQT. They key to doing well on the Critical Reading section is learning the different types of questions and how to answer them correctly.

It's not about how fast you can read the passages, but knowing how to distinguish the one right answer from the four wrong ones. The answers are generally found in the same place every time, and it's just a matter of learning how to find them.

This is an objective test, so Critical Reading questions can only have one right answer. The correct answer MUST be derived from the key words and clues from the sentence, not what you think the answer should be. The College Board writes answer choices intended to trap test-takers, but once you learn how to recognize these traps, you can answer the questions quickly and accurately.

Most students cringe at the thought of the Critical Reading section on the SAT and PSAT/NMSQT.

It's not about how fast you can read the passages, but knowing how to distinguish the one right answer from the four wrong ones.

Steps to Critical Reading Success:

1. Learn the strategy ACRONYMS*.
2. Memorize the root words and positive and negative prefixes found in the back of this book.
3. Read and understand the rules for this section before taking the real test.
4. Practice taking the Critical Reading section in College Board exams.

*The ACRONYMS are designed to help you remember the specific strategies for each section. While you are learning the ACRONYMS, feel free keep your notes open as you work practice problems. When you take a practice exam, get in the habit of writing the ACRONYM at the top of the paper.

During the actual SAT exam, you are not allowed to bring in any notes, but you are allowed to write in the booklet. (Do not write on the grid-in paper.) **This is why it's important to memorize the ACRONYMS!**

The ACRONYMS are designed to help you remember the specific strategies for each section.

FORMAT

The Critical Reading section comprises two sections:

- Passage-Based Reading
- Sentence Completion

PASSAGE-BASED READING

THE PASSAGE-BASED READINGS SECTION will give a passage discussing a particular topic which will be followed by several questions relating to the passage. It is not necessary to have a previous knowledge about the topics in the reading passages. Even if you if you're clueless about the subject at hand, don't worry! Every correct answer can be found **in** the text.

There are three types of passages:
- Long Passage
- Short Passage
- Dual Passage

For each passage type, there are generally three types of questions you will be given:
- Line Citation
- Vocabulary Use
- Overall Passage

All three types of questions are answered using different processes which will be discussed further in this chapter. Do NOT read all the questions first, then read the passage and then go back and read each question! This will waste time and confuse you. Reading the whole passage is not necessary. You do not need to be an expert on the passage, just have a basic understanding of it. Most of the information inside the reading passages is unnecessary.

It is not necessary to have a previous knowledge about the topics in the reading passages.

RECURRING PATTERNS AND STRATEGIES

OPINIONATED ANSWER CHOICES

If a question seems to ask your opinion, it is a trap. The questions are 100% objective which leaves no room for personal opinions.

If a question seems to ask your opinion, it is a trap. The questions are 100% objective which leaves no room for personal opinions. The right answers are ALWAYS objective—never subjective. There is ONLY one right answer and it can be found in the text.

If an answer it is too strong, too opinionated or negative toward a person/group of people, it is wrong. If an answer choice expresses a radical idea with no room for exceptions, this answer choice is wrong. You always want to avoid statements that seem to exclude all possibilities. Only choose answer choices that leave room for exceptions. Avoid answer choices with words like *exactly, always, all, every, must, no, none* and *never*.

Avoid answers that contain S.O.N.

S trong
O pinionated
N egative

To be politically correct, the good answer choices will usually contain words that cover all possibilities such as *often, if, mostly, usually, may, can, almost, sometimes* and *some*. For example:

Wrong Answer Choices:
It is never cold in December.
Post-Modernism paintings are always confusing.
Everyone in the military during the sixties needed psychological help.
None of the teachers liked their job.
Money only appeals to the rich.

Good Answer Choices:
Boys are usually tougher than girls.
It sometimes rains in the big city.

Eating too much fat will <u>probably</u> result in weight gain.

<u>Most</u> adult Americans own a car.

Women <u>often</u> work outside the home to supplement the family income.

The College Board will never express a negative opinion about a certain people group, ethnicity or world region. Any answer choice that puts a general population in a negative light will be incorrect.

Passages will always be positive that reference a people group. We know that NO answer choice will be correct if it puts a negative light on people. In Example 1-1 we can automatically mark off the negative answers (A), (C) & (E) because these are negative toward a group of people.

> ## Example 1-1
> In the passage, how did the people of the village view the foreign missionaries?
>> (A) intrusive
>> (B) helpful
>> (C) needy
>> (D) loving
>> (E) rude

This leaves only two answers (positive) to choose from; the correct one can be found in the key parts of the text. The correct answer may not seem perfect to you, but it is always the choice with the least wrong information and no hidden meanings or secretive agendas. Only the correct answers can be defended by The College Board.

WATCH OUT FOR EXCEPTIONS

If a question has the word "except" in it, like in Example 1-2, immediately circle the word. The word "except" means you are looking for any answer that does not appear in the passage.

Find all the answer choices that appropriately reference the text; then **mark them out!** These are obviously wrong. Choose the answer choice that isn't eliminated. There will only be one.

> ## Example 1-2
> The passage suggests all of the following <u>**except**</u>

ANSWERS WITH THE SAME MEANING

Remember, the test is objective and there can never be two correct answers. If two answers have the same meaning, they are both wrong.

Example 1-3

Line 16: The reporter was surprised by the brazen attitude the author had toward the critical reviews of his most recent novel.

8. What does the word "brazen" most nearly mean in Line 16?
   (A) Nonchalant
   (B) Irate
   (C) Grateful
   (D) Cheeky
   (E) Wrathful

In Example 1-3 if we look at the answer choices, we notice two synonyms: (B) Irate and (E) Wrathful. They both mean being full of anger. Neither of these answers could be correct because they have the same meaning. Since the test is objective, there can ONLY be one answer. They are both wrong. Mark them off! The correct answer is (D) Cheeky.

It is a good idea to jot a quick definition next to each word to help you identify its meaning. To minimize mistakes, NEVER work problems in your head.

FUN TIP

Sometimes when there are two answer choices that are opposites, one of them will usually be the correct answer.

ANSWER CHOICES THAT DON'T ANSWER THE QUESTION

Example 1-4

The author mentions the trainer he met at the dog show in order to show that…

An answer choice may be correct, but it may not appropriately answer the question.

For the above Example 1-4 you may have an answer choice like "(A) Siberian Huskies can withstand severe bitter cold so they often thrive in Canada as pets." This statement may be true and may be found in the passage, but it does not answer the question. The right choice MUST answer the question.

LINE CITATION QUESTIONS

The Line Citation Question type is when a question asks about a particular line in the reading passage and then gives you five answer choices. See Example 1-5.

Citation questions are usually in order of the passage, so they are easy to locate without having to read the entire passage first.

Example 1-5

The author refers to "my favorite place" in lines 21–22 in order to...

READ or SKIM?

It is NOT necessary to read the whole passage. You should be able to find the correct answer by going directly to the cited part of the passage. (*Always circle the citation.*) If you need a little more information, you can dig a little deeper by reading a few lines above or below the cited line. Remember, this is <u>not</u> a test about knowledge, but how well you can reason and get the correct answer.

Some students like to read the whole passage, while others only get confused by doing so. This is strictly a personal choice on what works best for you. Since most of the information in the passage is irrelevant to answering the questions, it is **NOT** necessary to read the entire passage. The SAT usually gives you the most important parts that they want you to know from the line citation questions and they are generally in relevant order.

WHAT TO LOOK FOR

You are looking for the answer that restates the citation, not a direct quote. The correct answer usually does not have the exact words, but gives more of a general idea. <u>If you do not find the correct information in the citation, think logically by looking right around the circled citation.</u>

WORK THE PENCIL

First, use the pencil to circle the citation in the passage. Then, circle the nouns and verbs in the citation. Next, circle the nouns and verbs in the answer choices. The one that has the most matching nouns and verbs is usually the correct answer.

FIRST WORDS

Always circle the first word in the answer choices. Very often it will point you to the right answer or help eliminate the wrong answers.

Example 1-6

Line 48: At the well as I sat meditating on what had just happened, I felt like I finally rid myself of all those fears that encompassed my childhood.

3. The narrator refers to "all those fears" in line 48 primarily in order to show that he was
   (A) celebrating his upbringing
   (B) instilling a truth about deep thoughts
   (C) recreating a joyous memory from school
   (D) shedding the trepidation that preoccupied him
   (E) preserving memories that consumed his life

Look at Example 1-6. By circling the key first word in each answer choice, we see that every choice has a very different meaning. Many of the first words do not even come close to fitting the meaning of the example sentence. "Celebrating," "Instilling," and "Preserving" do not fit the context, and in fact contradict the sentence, so we can mark them off without even reading the full answer choices. If we read answer choice (C), we notice the context of this sentence contradicts the example as well. Therefore **(D)** is the correct answer choice.

COATED WRONG ANSWERS

Your job is to look for Goldilocks answers: ones that are just right! Look for answers that don't contain too much, too little information or information that is different from the original citation. The College Board likes to **C.O.A.T.** the wrong answers with four hidden patterns:

C ompletely irrelevant
O bscure information
A dditional information
T otally contradictory information

Sometimes you can find the **ONE CORRECT ANSWER** by marking off the four incorrect answers. Always circle what the question is asking! When approaching a test question, circle the citation, circle the first words of the answer choices and then circle the nouns and verbs. As you go through the answer choices, write a "C," "O," "A," or "T" next to each incorrect answer choice, whichever applies. Read questions carefully and critically so that you don't fall for these four traps.

> ## Example 1-7
> Line 48: At the well as I sat meditating on what had just happened, I felt like I finally rid myself of all those fears that encompassed my childhood.
>
>   (D) shedding the trepidation that preoccupied him

Look at same Example 1-7. By simply circling the nouns and verbs in the citation and answer choices, it is much easier to find the correct answer. Notice how "rid," "fears," and "encompassed" almost perfectly mirror "shedding," "trepidation," and "preoccupied" in the correct answer choice.

If you are overthinking the question or second-guessing yourself, you are probably falling for a COATed answer. Do not read anything additional into the information. The passage has all the information you need to answer the question. Nothing added—nothing subtracted. Make sure that ALL words in your answer choice coincide with the line citation. If the passage states the sentence below:

> ## Example 1-8
> Previous studies have shown that many professional athletes file for bankruptcy within five years of retirement.

"Previous studies have shown that many professional athletes file for bankruptcy within five years of retirement." [Example 1-8]

A wrong answer might be: like Example 1-9

Example 1-9

(A) Most former football players have created a lifestyle that is hard to maintain long after retirement.

This answer choice reads too much into the citation and adds to the text. The second statement may be true, but it is not supported by the original sentence. The original sentence says professional athletes (not former football players) file for bankruptcy (not necessarily because of their lifestyle) within five years (which may or may not be long after retirement).

SIMPLIFY BIG WORDS

Example 1-10

The author's main purpose for mentioning Ken's apathy when David forgot his backpack was to emphasize the
  (A) erratic way school supplies are used
  (B) dualistic personality of Ken
  (C) zeal that David felt
  (D) foretelling of a recurring event
  (E) comparison of Ken's effervescence to David's amazement

Advanced vocabulary words are often used to confuse the meaning of the answer choices. One strategy for helping you find the right answer is simplifying the big word to something easier to understand. Substitute everyday normal words for hard words and write them above the answer choices. You may also want to rewrite the answer choice to make more sense.

Let's simplify these answer choices in Example 1-10 by rewriting them. You only need to mark out the big words and write the easier word next to them.

(A) **erratic** way school supplies are used
Changing the use of the backpack—C, this is totally irrelevant.

(B) **dualistic** personality of Ken
Ken has **two** personalities—O, this is obscure information.

(C) **zeal** that David felt

David was **passionate**—A, this adds additional information.

(D) **foretelling** of a recurring event
Predicting a usual act—CORRECT, fits the sentence because the event was no surprise.

(E) comparison of Ken's **effervescence** to David's amazement
Comparing Ken's **light-heartedness** to David's excitement—T, this contradicts the sentence.

Rewording the sentence it make finding the correct answer much easier.

APPOSITIVES (RENAMING THE NOUN)

An appositive sets off a nonessential part of the sentence and also renames the noun.

My brother, Bill, is a doctor.

Bill and doctor describe the same person. By understanding this in a passage question, it will be easier to answer it. See Example 1-11

Your goal in this question is to find a phrase that restates "made a mistake." From the answer choices, we see that **(E)** restates this idea, and it is the correct answer.

Example 1-11

She made a mistake, a slip of the tongue, when it was her turn.

The phrase "slip of the tongue" refers to which of the following?
  (A) a political misunderstanding
  (B) a discerned comment
  (C) a failed attempt to adapt
  (D) a misconception of facts
  (E) a faux pas utterance

LINE CITATION EXAMPLE

Below is an example (1-12) of how to properly work a Line Citation question using the COAT strategy:

Example 1-12

In line 23, what was the author describing?

Line 23 The girl sat at the church praying to God about politics.

(A) The priest had strict policies about mixing religion and politics.

(B) Praying in the church about politics is prohibited during the week.

(C) When female parishioners pray, they are supposed to cover their heads.

(D) The beautiful stained glass windows help inspire a more thoughtful praying time for the people.

(E) The girl's religion and political interests were often in her prayers to God.

Start by finding the cited part of the passage (e.g., line 23) and **circle** it. Then read it and **circle** the nouns and verbs. Proceed to the answer choices and **circle** all the nouns and verbs. If the question asks about a particular line and it is in the middle of a sentence, go to the beginning and read the sentence in its entirety. If the line citation starts with a pronoun like *they, it, those, etc.,* you need to go backward and identify who or what the pronoun represents.

After circling the nouns and verbs (*girl, sat, church, praying, God, politics*), you find the correct answer choice has "religion, God, political interest" in it. If you haven't found the right answer yet, try to eliminate the wrong answer choices—those that have been COATed with hidden tricks. When you find one, cross it out and write a **"C," "O," "A,"** or **"T"** by it.

This will also help in case you accidentally cross out all five answer choices. If this happens, go back and read the lines around the citation. Any answer choice that has an **A (Additional Information)** marked by it, could be the correct answer (with other surrounding information in it). The correct answer should restate the main points in the citation.

Read carefully, critically and conscientiously.

Here's an ACRONYM to help you remember the process for answering Line Citation questions:

C ircle the citation in the passage
I dentify nouns/verbs—circle them
T erminate hidden patterns
A dditional information
T otally contradictory information
I rrelevant information
O bscure information
N ote the one that restates

Write **CITATION** at the top of your test page during practice and on the actual SAT booklet.

The correct answer will restate the important elements of the line citation. Read each answer critically and with great scrutiny to find the correct one.

Nothing Added—Nothing Omitted! No Addition—No Subtraction!

USE OF VOCABULARY QUESTIONS

This type of question will ask you to define the use of a vocabulary word in a sentence. The most common definition of the word is usually an answer choice. However, it is usually the WRONG answer. The correct answer will fit grammatically, make the most sense and go with the context of the sentence.

In the above Example 1-13, when one thinks about "charges", the definition "costs" comes to mind first. As mentioned above, this is a trap. We can mark it off because it doesn't fit this sentence. The way to find the correct answer is by <u>U</u>nquestionably <u>S</u>ubstituting <u>E</u>ach answer choice in the sentence. Write acronym **USE** at the top of the test page.

Example 1-13

The word "charges" in line 27 most nearly means…

Line 27 The shop foreman had heavy charges put upon him with the new load of responsibilities.
  (A) costs
  (B) minds
  (C) burdens
  (D) innocence
  (E) judges

U nquestionably
S ubstitute
E ach answer choice in the sentence

FUN TIP

If there are two answer choices that are similar in meaning, then they are both wrong because the test leaves no room for subjectivity.

If we insert each answer choice into the example sentence, we find that B, D and E do not fit. C is the correct answer because it makes the most sense and fits grammatically.

If you find a Scope word see 86 (SCOPE words) in the vocabulary use question, circle it. This will change the positive/negative flow of direction. Remember, the word "And" connects (same flow) and "Or" contradicts (changes flow).

OVERALL PASSAGE QUESTIONS

This question type asks about the entire passage. Overall Passage Questions include five main types of problems:

Tone—determining the predominate mood of the passage—whether it's positive or negative, mysterious, neutral (*What tone does the author take? How did the villagers feel?*).

Main Idea—discovering the important thought or main purpose from the author (*What is the author's primary thought? What is the passage's main purpose?*).

Inferences—deciding what is implied by the author and drawing inferences beyond the literal explanation and deriving a correct conclusion from the given details (*What is the author suggesting? What is the author implying?*).

Details—detecting and identifying specific information from the given text/citations (*In Line 4, what is she describing? Who is responsible (in Line 16) for...?*).

Comparison—determining the difference between two points of view (*How would the author of Passage 2 respond to the last sentence in Passage 1? Which statement would best fit Passage 2 and not Passage 1?*).

This question type is usually the first question in the passage section. This is because most students answer questions in a row starting with question one. But on these tests, this can waste a ton of time causing you to read through the passage several times in order to try and answer it. **PASS** these questions up until you have answered all the other question types first. Put a star by them so you don't forget to come back and answer them. You don't necessarily have to read the entire passage, but you do need a general overview.

The College Board has given you the main points already in the other question types that you've already answered. Most of the passage is unnecessary to know.

When you come across an overall passage question, go back and do the essential reading: the italicized introduction (underline it), all the circled citations, the opening sentence of each paragraph (underline it) and the closing sentence of each paragraph (underline it). By going over these parts, you should be able to infer the answer to the question. If the question is about tone, this simple exercise should show you whether the overall tone is either positive or negative. Even if there are parts with negative information, if the overall the passage is positive, then your answer will be positive.

Use basic reasoning to mark off the wrong answers and pick the one that hints or implies the right answer. Every single word in the correct answer will be right! It will usually be politically correct, contain no harsh words and will not distort the truth. Avoid **S.O.N.** (**S**trong, **O**pinionated, **N**egative) choices.

Write the acronym PASSAGE at the top of your page:

P
A } these questions up until the end
S
S
A dd the essential reading
G o over the circled portions/answers
E very word is nice and politically correct in the correct answer

LONG AND SHORT READING PASSAGE

The Short Passage and the Long Passage are very similar to one another. They both contain the three main question types: Line Citation, Vocabulary Use and Overall Passage. You can use all the same strategies for answering the questions on both.

The only difference is that the Long Passage contains multiple paragraphs (around 110 lines) while the Short Passage generally only contains one.

Since the short passage is usually one paragraph, <u>the Overall Passage answers are probably found in the first and last sentences.</u>

DUAL READING PASSAGE

This section contains two separate passages followed by several questions. The two passages are usually connected by the same common topic. They may be giving opposing or harmonious points of view. Always note (write in the booklet) whether the passages agree, disagree or complement one another. This can often be reflected in the italicized part. <u>Always read and underline the italicized portion of both passages first.</u> (Very often, an answer can be found in the italicized section.) As a general rule, if the two passages seem to have a different subject matter, they probably agree on a unifying theme. If they are both speaking on the same subject, they probably disagree.

Passage 1 and Passage 2 are next to each other on purpose for you to read them both together and then answer the questions. (*This is a trap!*) Don't fall for the way they have set up this section. Skim the first passage and answer just its questions, and <u>then</u> do the second passage and its questions. Circle the citations and look for the answers in or near them. PASS up the Overall Passage questions about <u>both</u> passages until the end. Underline the main theme of each passage. By reading the circled citations, first and last sentences of each paragraph and the italicized opening, you can get the main theme and answer the overall passage questions.

For answering questions about both passages, underline pertinent information in each passage. (For example, if one passage is "for" something and the other is "against" it, make a note next to each passage so you won't confuse the passages.) *Know what each passage is talking about.*

BOTH PASSAGE TRAPS

1. Beware of answers that sidetrack or confuse you.
    This is why it is important to do one passage at a time.
2. Watch out for answers that neglect one passage altogether.
    This is where an answer choice only relects one passage instead of both.
3. Sometimes the answer choices swap passages.
    An answer choice gives information from the other passage or changes person from the other passage.

Example 1-14

What (negative) feature does (each) passage stress?

(A) Passage 1 discusses political ~~harmony~~ and Passage 2 discusses critical analysis.

(B) Passage 1 discusses dissension in the ranks and Passage 2 discusses ~~peaceful unity~~.

(C) Passage 1 discusses ~~tranquil being~~ and Passage 2 discusses rude awakening.

(D) Passage 1 discusses discord among brotherhood and Passage 2 discusses harsh judgment.

(E) Passage 1 discusses deliberate strife and Passage 2 discusses severe ranking.

Always circle what the question is asking! Often times, the question has several criteria that need to be answered, and by knowing this, wrong answers can be immediately spotted.

In Example 1-14 by circling the two criteria (negative and each), we can quickly eliminate answers with the wrong patterns. If any answer choice contains any positive words, mark them out. With the remaining answers, make sure that they are found in each passage. Remember that the answer choices often switch passages or ignore one passage altogether.

Here's an acronym to help you memorize the process for doing DUAL Passage questions:

D o each passage and questions one at a time
U nderline main themes in each passage
A nswers must match correct passage
L eave both passage questions till the end

Write DUAL at the top of your page, on the Dual Passage section.

SENTENCE COMPLETION

THIS TYPE OF QUESTION in the Critical Reading section will present a complete sentence with either one or two blanks in it. Your goal is to find the perfect word to fit in the blank or blanks. There will be five answer choices to choose from.

At first, this seems to be merely a section that quizzes vocabulary skills. If you knew all the words in the answer choice, you would easily be able to decipher the correct answer. Many students approach this section by learning lots of vocabulary words. Although this is a good practice and will help with overall communication abilities, knowing thousands of words does not guarantee a good score on this section.

What if you get to the test and can't find any of the words you have learned? This is a very real possibility. Fortunately, The College Board has a certain profile and pattern that they use when they write their questions. Every question can be figured out without prior knowledge of all the words in the answer choices. This section of the book is designed to help you discover the correct answer through a few specific strategies.

THE POSITIVE/NEGATIVE TEST

Many unknown words can be figured out if you apply the Positive/Negative Test. What is your first impression of the unknown word? Say the word and listen to the sound of it. If it seems to have a good meaning, then it is probably a **positive** word with a good connotation. When you listen to the sound of the word and it seems to have a bad meaning, then it is probably a **negative** word with a bad connotation.

See if you can figure out by the sound of these words whether they're positive or negative. What is your first thought on the word? After you take this test, look up the actual definitions in the dictionary and see if your first impression was correct.

Word	Positive	Negative
Sycophant	_____	_____
Tedium	_____	_____
Decorous	_____	_____
Timorous	_____	_____
Expunge	_____	_____
Florid	_____	_____
Lurid	_____	_____
Pacificator	_____	_____
Querulous	_____	_____
Pinion	_____	_____
Quintessential	_____	_____
Ribald	_____	_____
Licentious	_____	_____

Example 1-15

The angry man _____ out of the store as he _____ grabbed his bag of groceries.

When taking the test, predict if the word in the blank will be positive or negative. Write a P (positive) or N (negative) in the blank. Above the P or N, write a word that might fit. Then find answer choices that give the sentence the same pattern of negatives and positives. See if the words are closely related to the word(s) you wrote. Try this for yourself in Example 1-15.

The above sentence is negative, and there's no change in direction, so both answers will be negative. If we tried to predict the words, they would probably be along the line of *stormed* and *hurriedly*. Now look at the answer choices and find the two words that are negative and have a close meaning to "stormed" and "hurriedly."

(A) walked…carefully
(B) marched…sympathetically

(C) ambulated...tenderly

(D) strolled...violently

(E) stamped...aggressively

In (A), both words are positive. In (B) and (C), the second word is positive. In (D), the first word is positive. In (E), both words are negative and close to the words we predicted. Therefore, answer **(E)** is correct.

Answers from page 84 (N, N, P, N, N, P, N, P, N, N, P, N, N)

ROOTS AND PREFIXES ARE IMPORTANT!

Latin roots, cognates and derivatives are useful tools for deriving the meaning of an unknown word. Another way to apply the positive/negative test is to learn prefixes, because many are either positive or negative. Sometimes just the beginning or ending of a word can point you to the correct answer.

Although Example 1-16 appears difficult, it's actually just testing your reasoning skills as usual. Since there is a comma, the flow of the sentence stays the same and the key to the blank is found before the comma. We are looking for a word that describes the "autobiographers freedom and separation". (A) and (C) are unknown words—skip them. (B) is an unknown word that sounds negative and doesn't fit. (D) is a negative prefix ("not noble")—mark it off. (E) is an unknown word, but "sage" means wisdom—mark it off. (A) and (D) have been skipped, but notice the words "autobiographer" and "autonomy" both have the same prefix, so **(C)** is correct.

> ## Example 1-16
> The autobiographer's book was all about freedom and separation from the norm. Her _____ was prevalent throughout every page.
> (A) serendipity
> (B) waspishness
> (C) autonomy
> (D) ignobility
> (E) sagaciousness

Learn the positive and negative prefixes, root words and suffices found in appendix A (page 260). Mark down when you know them and then write and learn several new words that use them.

KEY ELEMENTS

Sentence Completion answers should not be based on what you think sounds good (especially since several answers may fall into that category), but based on the key elements found in the sentence that point you to the answer.

SCOPE WORDS

These are words you will "SCOPE" out to see if they are in the sentence. These are words such as *not, unlike, although, but, while, rather, in spite, however, despite, nonetheless, whereas, on the other hand, nevertheless, by contrast,* and *yet.*

If you find these words, the flow of the sentence will change from positive to negative or from negative to positive. Generally you're looking for a word that's opposite of the other half of the sentence with a Scope word. Try it for yourself in Example 1-17.

First, circle the SCOPE word "but." This changes the flow of the sentence, which starts out positive. You're not only looking for a negative answer, but one that is the opposite of "happy." Mark off the positive answers (A) and (C). (D) is negative, but it's not the opposite of happy. (E) is an unknown word, but because (B) is a perfect fit, it doesn't matter what "plebeian" means (*plebeian* means common).

Sometimes when you find a SCOPE word, it doesn't necessarily mean both answer choices will be opposite. It <u>does</u> mean there is a flow change, but sometimes the contrast can be found in other parts of the sentence. See Example 1-18

Example 1-17

Suzanne was always a happy child, but she became _____ when she turned ten.

 (A) joyous
 (B) depressed
 (C) lovable
 (D) rebellious
 (E) plebeian

Example 1-18

The historical organization _____ the nightly news for prominently reporting the so-called UFO sightings while _____ to cover a stellar archeological find.

 (A) praised...declining
 (B) celebrated...hurrying
 (C) dismissed...embracing
 (D) criticized...failing
 (E) honoring...electing

This example sentence contains the SCOPE word **"while."** This tells us that there is a flow change somewhere. When we look at the first half of the sentence, we see the words "prominently reporting." This is a positive phrase, so the second blank will be negative because it reflects the opposite of this phrase. Obviously this organization disliked the reporting because they say it's "so-called," which means the first word will also be negative.

Even though there is a flow change in this sentence, we will be looking for two answers that are negative. It would be a good idea to first circle "while" and then put a "P" above "prominently reporting." Then draw an arrow from the "P" to the first blank, where you will put an "N."

Notice that (A) and (B) are positive/negative, (C) is negative/positive and (E) is positive/positive. **(D)** is the only answer that is negative/negative—and by looking at the context, we see that this sentence is negative overall (with a positive phrase to satisfy the SCOPE word).

Predict the Word for the Following Sentences That Contain a Scope Word Don't forget to circle the SCOPE word:

1. Even though they are a small group, dolphin activists have had a _____ impact on preserving dignity for sea mammals.
2. The neighbor's dog had always been friendly, but he suddenly became _____ when his owner left him alone.
3. I found the carwash attendant very rude, however when I saw him at church he seemed _____.

You may have come up with words like: "large/great" for question 1, "mean/vicious" for question 2 and "polite/friendly" for question 3. As long as your predicted word implies the opposite of the other half of the sentence, it's a good prediction.

COMMAS, COLONS AND SEMICOLONS

Commas, colons and semicolons by themselves keep the sentence flow the same. If it starts negative, it will remain negative; if it starts positive, it will remain positive. The correct answer will restate a portion of the other half of the sentence that's separated by the colon or semicolon (the part without the blank).

To solve these, cut the sentence in half with your pencil at the comma, colon or semicolon. Then, draw an arrow from the blank to the word(s) it describes.

Example 1-19

Bill was lacking in skills and was very unqualified for the top position; his _____ had once again kept him from the promotion.

    (A) capability
    (B) personality
    (C) trumpery
    (D) incompetence
    (E) humility

In Example 1-19 circling the semicolon in this sentence reminds you that the flow of the sentence will stay the same. Since the first half is negative, you're looking for a negative word that helps describe the first half of the sentence. Cut the sentence in half and draw an arrow to the word(s) you want to describe (*lacking in skills*). Mark off the positive answers (A) and (E). (B) is neutral, so it's wrong. (C) is an unknown word (*trumpery* means junk), but we don't have to know its meaning because **(D)** fits the sentence perfectly. Remember, only one word will fit perfectly, so once we find it, the remaining answer choices don't matter.

Example 1-20

The brilliant professor was known for his _____ speeches.

    (A) luminous
    (B) boring
    (C) lunatic
    (D) uneducable
    (E) garbled

ADJECTIVES/ADVERBS

If there is no SCOPE word or comma/colon/semicolon in the sentence, sometimes the adjectives or adverbs can point you to the right answer. In Example 1-20 we know the sentence doesn't contain a change in negative/positive flow, so whether the adjectives are positive or negative, the blank will follow suit. Magnify the adjectives by circling them and mark above it a **"P"** if it is positive and an **"N"** if it is negative.

Since the adjective "brilliant" is positive and there is no SCOPE word, the answer will be positive. Mark off (B) and (C) because they are obviously negative answers. (D) must be negative because of the prefix "un," and (E) sounds negative. **(A)** is the correct answer.

CAUSE AND EFFECT WORDS

Sentences that don't contain a SCOPE word sometimes contain Cause and Effect Words. These words can be found in sentences with the same flow. They show a cause and effect relationship between two parts of the sentence. Circle these words if you find them in the prompt sentence.

hence, therefore, so, then, consequently, accordingly, when, because, thus, etc.

These words demonstrate a consequence, result or outcome between the two parts of the sentence.

For Example 1-21, first, circle the semicolon and then circle "therefore." Then draw an arrow from the Cause and Effect Word to the phrase that starts the action and requires a result ("overstrained her calf muscles"). We can predict that the blank will probably be a word like "replaced." The correct answer is **(C) substituted**.

> ## Example 1-21
> Leslie overstrained her calf muscles during a workout; therefore, her place on the team was _____ by an alternate sprinter.
> (A) secured
> (B) distinguished
> (C) substituted
> (D) dismissed
> (E) examined

STRENGHTENING WORDS

Sometimes sentences that do not have a SCOPE word will contain Strengthening Words. They help strengthen the correct word choice and can point you to the correct answer. Strengthening Words keep the same flow and continue the logic. Circle these words if you find them in the prompt sentence:

so, since, besides, also, in fact, furthermore, too, moreover, in addition, as well, indeed, additionally, etc.

Strengthening Words usually support the first half of the sentence. Draw an arrow from the Strengthening Word or phrase to the phrase that it supports. Choose the answer choice that strengthens this phrase.

Example 1-22

Many scientists agree with the creation theory; in fact, they often _____ it in their speeches.

   (A) disavow
   (B) pamper
   (C) exploit
   (D) acknowledge
   (E) debar

In Example 1-22, first, circle the comma and then circle "in fact." Then draw an arrow from the Strengthening Word to the word it's strengthening ("agree"). From the answer choices only answer choice **(D) acknowledge** serves to strengthen the first half of the sentence.

ONE BLANK SENTENCE COMPLETION

The first thing you should do when you approach a sentence completion question is predict the blank. Don't look at the answer choices! This will bias your judgment, so cover them up.

Determine the context of the sentence to see whether the word in the blank will be positive or negative. Then think of a word that fits and makes logical sense in context. Now, look at the answer choices and find the one that's similar to the word you predicted.

PREDICT THE WORD FOR THE FOLLOWING SENTENCES:

1. Most new gourmet dishes are not created overnight; as a matter of fact, their debut is usually a _____ process.

2. The justice division of some government offices is there to _____ the unfair treatment of employees by their supervisors.

3. The constant need to expand storage space shows that his business venture is off to a _____ start.

You may have come up with words like *tedious* or *long* for question 1, *prevent* or *stop* for question 2 and *good* or *successful* for question 3. It doesn't matter what your predicted word is, as long as it's similar to these. If you had a hard time predicting a good word, look for the key elements that will help show you how to find the correct answer for each of these questions.

TWO-BLANK SENTENCE COMPLETION

The two-blank Sentence Completion questions are identical to the one-blank question except that they contain two blanks. All the same rules and strategies apply, but keep in mind that both words MUST fit exactly.

One of The College Board's tricks is to make one of the words a PERFECT word. It's usually the most common word used in that context. However, the second word will NOT work. Don't force it to fit. This is a trap! You can usually MARK OUT two to three answer choices right off the bat by eliminating choices that contain one word that will not fit.

In Example 1-23 first, we notice the SCOPE word "in spite." This tells us that the flow of the sentence will change. Predict the first blank. It will probably be a positive word, (like "good") which makes the second blank negative. Two approaches work for answering the two-blank sentences.

(1) Mark off all answers that have a negative first word—(A) and (C). Next, mark off answers that contain a positive second word—(B) and (D).

Example 1-23
In spite of his _____ intentions, Greg's New Year's resolutions were soon _____ shortly after making them.
    (A) peculiar…derailed
    (B) good…advanced
    (C) lousy…finished
    (D) acrimonious…encouraged
    (E) worthwhile…hindered

(2) The other way to find the answer is to mark off all answers that don't have a positive/negative flow. Either way, we easily find our answer, which is (E).

Notice that (B) "good" was the PERFECT word. This is a trap because the second word did not fit.

Sometimes you can find the answer by starting with the <u>second blank first</u>. Very often by solving the second blank first, the answer for the first blank will fall into place, especially if there are SCOPE words. Check out Example 1-24

Example 1-24

The early reviews of the newest animated film came out _____, despite the fact that it _____ previous box office successes.

   (A) mixed...surpassed
   (B) raving...achieved
   (C) poorly....floundered
   (D) pulchritudinous...matched
   (E) unfavorable...foreshadowed

When you look at the first part of the sentence, there are no clues to whether the first blank is positive or negative, so we have to start with the second blank <u>first.</u> Notice the SCOPE word "despite," and circle it. This means the first blank has to be opposite of the second blank. We can see from the word "successes" that the second word will be positive; therefore, the first word will be negative. From this positive/negative mix, we discover that only **(A)** can be correct since: (B) contains two positive words (C) the second word is negative (D) first word is unknown and the second word doesn't fit (E) the second word doesn't fit.

ANSWER CHOICE TRAPS

IMPOSTER WORDS

Sometimes the makers of the SAT will put imposter words in the answer choices to confuse students. Often these wrong answer choices look very similar to the perfect answer, but beware! They are often with a completely different meaning—for example, the word "temporal" in place of the word "temperament."

illusion vs. allusion; uninterested vs. disinterested; optimal vs. optimistic

Look at Example 1-25. Your first thought might be to look for a word like *despondent*, and *despot* looks similar, but it has a completely different meaning; so, (A) is incorrect. Since the answer will be negative, (C) and (E) are out. (B) doesn't fit, so **(D)** the unknown word "forlorn" is correct. (It means *despondent* or *hopeless*.)

> ## Example 1-25
> After searching for days for her wedding ring, Janice became _____ and just gave up.
> (A) despot
> (B) intrigued
> (C) hopeful
> (D) forlorn
> (E) carefree

SAME SUBJECT AREA

Watch out for answer choices that have a similar subject area as the sentence. This is usually a trap. Although the answer choice seems to fit the context of the sentence, it will usually be unrelated to the correct answer. See Example 1-26.

Since the sentence contains the word "political," it could be tempting to pick *partisanship* because it's in the same subject area—but (A) is incorrect. It doesn't fit the sentence properly. We need something that restates the portion of the sentence on the other side of the colon. It will be a positive word. (B) and (E) are negative, and (C) doesn't fit. **(D)** restates the second half of the sentence: *depth of perception and intuition.*

> ## Example 1-26
> John Adams' right-hand man was known for his political _____: his depth of perception and intuition were often called upon.
> (A) partisanship
> (B) indifference
> (C) prosperity
> (D) discernment
> (E) disobedience

UNKNOWN WORDS

Example 1-27
Despite the fact that many Chinese women in the late eighteenth century had very little say over the ritual of foot binding, Wan Bai Jie's memoirs exhibit an amazing amount of

_____.

(A) dedication
(B) justification
(C) silence
(D) autarchy
(E) tolerance

If you come across an unknown word in the answer choices, don't automatically rule it out or automatically pick it. Put a question mark next to it, pass it up and test all the other answers first. The unknown words are unimportant if you've already found the right answer. If you find the correct answer, then you can confidently mark off the unknown word. If none of the known words fit, simply choose the unknown word. *There is ALWAYS only one correct answer.* Try Example 1-27.

The SCOPE word "despite" (flow of sentence changes) tells us that the answer will be opposite of "very little say." (A) and (B) are positive and don't fit. (C) means "to erase," so it doesn't fit. (D) is an unknown word—skip it. (E) doesn't change the flow. This leaves only the unknown word "autarchy," which is correct. (It means *self-governed*.)

CONTRADICTORY WORDS

Example 1-28
Devon felt very _____ after he received the gloomy proposal regarding his bid.

Very often one of the answer choices will be the exact opposite of the correct answer choice. If the correct answer is the word "ecstatic," the word "miserable" may be an answer choice.

In Example 1-28, the answer will be negative because the adjective "gloomy" points us to the correct answer choice, so a word like *melancholy* could work—but, the answer choices may contain an opposite answer like *optimistic*.

SENTENCE COMPLETION PROCESS

1. **C**lassify words you don't know when you read the prompt sentence. This means that you should <u>underline</u> any word whose meaning you don't know.

2. **O**perate the Positive/Negative test on the <u>underlined</u> words. Again, this means to think about the word. If the word seems like it has a good meaning, then it is probably a positive word with a good connotation. If it seems bad, then it is probably a negative word.

3. **M**agnify any KEY ELEMENTS in the sentence. If any of these are present, <u>circle</u> them darkly to remind you how to find the correct answer.

> SCOPE WORDS—change the flow of the sentence
> COLONS/SEMICOLONS/COMMAS—keep the same flow
> ADJECTIVES/ADVERBS—point you to the answer
> CAUSE AND EFFECT WORDS—show the result
> STRENGHTENING WORDS—support the flow

4. **P**redict whether the blank(s) require positive or negative words. You can determine this by knowing all the words in the prompt sentence, (positive/ negative test), by the magnified SCOPE words and by the adjectives. Predict the word-write it in the blank.

5. **L**ook at the answer choices.

6. **E**liminate the wrong flow answer choices that do not fit the pattern of the prompt sentence.

<u>Example</u>: If the blanks call for two positive words, and an answer choice has a negative word, you can feel assured when eliminating that answer choice.

7. **T**ry the second blank first. If you can't predict the first blank in a two-blank Sentence Completion question, go to the second blank. There should

be a hint in that section so you can answer it first. Then you should be able to answer the first blank.

8. **I**dentify the correct answer.

9. **O**nly one answer restates something in the prompt sentence or has the right flow of the sentence. Two answers with similar definitions are both wrong.

10. **N**ow it is an exact fit.

Here's an acronym to help you memorize the process of sentence completion:

C lassify unknown words
O perate the Positive/Negative test
M agnify KEY elements
P redict blank(s)—positive or negative
L ook at the answer choices
E liminate wrong flow answer choices
T ry the second blank first
I dentify the correct answer
O nly one restates
N ow it is an exact fit

Write COMPLETION at the top of your test page when you start the Critical Reading section.

PART III:

THE MATH SECTION

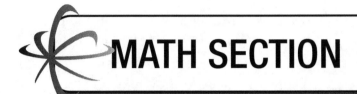

MATH SECTION

THE MATH SECTION OF the SAT and PSAT/NMSQT is NOT a math test. Math is only the vehicle being used to test a student's reasoning skills. This section requires students to THINK. Sometimes you are thinking in extremes—large, small, opposite, backwards—but you must think the questions all the way through in order to get them correct.

This portion of the test can be defined as a test of math terms, definitions and properties; this is why it is so important to make sure you know each of these that are found in this book. There is a glossary of math terms that you MUST know in Appendix B (page 277-302)

Each math question has an easy answer, and the key is to find the easy solution to each problem. You don't have to be a math genius! There is no calculus, trigonometry or college-level math on these tests. All you have to do is learn to look at the questions logically and understand how to <u>set up the problems</u> to find the correct answer. Most questions are simpler than you think.

The SAT math is not hard because it tests unknown or tough concepts, but it can be hard because the questions are designed to trick the students. If a student knows the basic math concepts, then the key to answering the questions is memorizing how to work each problem type. Most mistakes come from these areas:

- Carelessness—rushing or not realizing what the question was really asking
- Incorrect Problem Solving—missing a part of the steps or doing it in your head
- Falling for the Tricks—not reading with a critical eye

The math section of the SAT and PSAT/ NMSQT is NOT a math test.

The SAT math is not hard because it tests unknown or tough concepts, but it can be hard because the questions are designed to trick the students.

If you are taking a long time to work each problem, you are probably doing it the wrong way.

If you are taking a long time to work each problem, you are probably doing it the wrong way. Every math question can be solved two ways: in a long, tedious way or a short, direct way. There are shortcuts for every type of math problem on the SAT. There is no need to show all your work since this will cost you time. It's a good idea to familiarize yourself with all the shortcuts outlined in this section. Not only can you cut your time in half with shortcuts, but you can also avoid dumb mistakes with the less work you do.

Reading questions with a critical eye is very important. The questions are written in a way that isn't as clear as it could be, but in fact, it's more of a hindrance to the reader. Students need to learn to decode the questions. Even though each question contains all the necessary information, many times you will have to be a detective to locate the right information. Solving a hard question can simply be a matter of working several easy steps to get the answer.

The best way to do this is always work the problems in the booklet. NEVER try to do them in your head. Even shortcuts should be written out to help you derive the correct answer. Rewrite the problems if they are confusing to make them clearer.

Understanding the language is imperative to doing well on this section.

Understanding the language is imperative to doing well on this section. Math vocabulary is very important to know; otherwise, it will be difficult to answer many of the questions correctly. For example: *The word "positive" does not mean "even only," and zero is never positive.*

Keep in mind that all the math formulas used in this section can found at the beginning of the real test. If you forget how to work a certain problem, the answer can be derived by using one of these formulas. The formulas for area, circumference, and volume are all included at the front of the test, and you could use them to work problems that include cubes, prisms, cylinders, cones, spheres, pyramids, rectangular solids, etc.

Solving math questions requires four steps:

> **Decide**—What are they telling me in the question? (It probably needs to be rephrased because the language is a bit obscure.)

Decode —What is the bottom line? (Circle what they're really asking so you stay on track.)

Disguised—What answer do they want me to fall for? (They have cleverly hidden the real answer in an attempt to lead you toward the "dummy" answers.)

Declare —What should I really be thinking? (Knowing how to answer each question correctly comes from understanding the recurring patterns, so PRACTICING is essential.)

FUN TIP

Learn to SEE the math and not do the math.

STEPS TO MATH SUCCESS

1. Learn the Acronyms
2. Know the 300+ Math Terms in the back of this book
3. Read and understand the rules for this section before taking the real test
4. Practice the Math Section in actual College Board Tests

Remember, the SAT and PSAT are tests of logic and reasoning. You can use a calculator, and the math formulas are on the test. It is **EXTREMELY IMPORTANT** that you know what the math words mean and how to apply basic math concepts. More than 300 math vocabulary words and their definitions are included in the back of this book. Go over all the math vocabulary and corresponding definitions. Make sure you know ALL of them. Check them off if you know them, and learn the "ones you do not know.

Learn to look at each math problem logically. Learn the shortcuts and unique strategies that can unravel the hidden patterns on the math section. Memorize the ACRONYMS to help you remember these steps. While you are learning the ACRONYMS, keep your notes open to remind you of what each letter stands for. Get in the habit of writing the ACRONYMS at the top of your paper. During the actual SAT test, you are not allowed to bring any notes, but you are allowed to write in the booklet. (Do not write on the grid-in paper.) This is why it is important to **memorize** the ACRONYMS.

Remember, the SAT and NMSQT are tests of logic and reasoning.

THERE ARE TWO SECTIONS:

- Multiple Choice
- Student Response

MULTIPLE CHOICE:

The SAT math problems are often a combination of more than one concept.

This section contains a question followed by five answer choices.

The SAT math problems are often a combination of more than one concept. Make sure you not only understand the basic math but also the math terms, definitions and properties. Below are actual groups and subgroups that were found on recent, actual College Board math questions:

Number Properties & Operations	Algebra	Functions
Integer properties	Basic operations	Notation
Word problems— arithmetic	Factoring	Evaluate
Number lines	Exponents	Domain & range
Squares & square roots	Roots	Special symbols
Fractions & rationals	Equations	Functions as models
Primes, remainders, factors, multiples	Absolute value	Slope, linear equations
Ratios, percents, proportions	Phrase as math expression	Quadratic graphs
Sequences	Inequalities	Translations
Sets	Systems of equations & inequalities	
Counting problems	Rational equations & inequalities	
Logic	Variation	
	Word problems— algebraic	

<u>Geometry</u>

Points & lines
Angles—intersection & parallel
　lines
Triangles
　　　a)　special shapes
　　　b)　right angles and
　　　　　Pythagorean Th.
　　　c)　30–60-90 & 45–45–90
　　　d)　side ratios
　　　e)　congruent
　　　f)　similar
Quadrilaterals
Polygons
　　　a)　square & rectangle area
　　　b)　square & rectangle
　　　　　perimeter
　　　c)　triangle area &
　　　　　perimeter
　　　d)　other parallelograms
Polygon angles, area, perimeter
Circle area & circumference
Solids: volume, surface area
Coordinate Geometry
　　　a)　slope
　　　b)　midpoint
　　　c)　distance
　　　d)　transformation

<u>Statistics & Probability & Data</u>
<u>Interpretation</u>

Mean
Median
Mode
Weighted average & average of
　expressions
Probability
Graphs
　　　a)　circle
　　　b)　line
　　　c)　bar
　　　d)　picto-
　　　e)　scatter

BASIC STRATEGIES

NO CALCUATOR NEEDED

Always bring your calculator to the SAT and PSAT/NMSQT.

ALWAYS BRING YOUR CALCULATOR to the SAT and PSAT/NMSQT. Make sure it has square roots and exponent functions along with fresh batteries. However, most questions on the SAT should never need a calculator. Often times these devices only slow down the process of computing. Remember, your goal is to find the fastest way to answer the question. Not to mention, the more calculations you do on the calculator, the more chances you have of making a mistake. By learning how to not even turn it on, you can eliminate steps and save time. Try for yourself in Example 2-1.

Example 2-1

The area of each shaded square is 12. What is the total area of the non-shaded circles?

(A) $12\pi - 12$
(B) $24 - 12$
(C) $36 - 12$
(D) $3\pi - 36$
(E) $18\pi - 36$

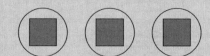

Let's look at what the question is really saying. The answer will be the area of the shaded squares subtracted from the non-shaded circles. In other words, the correct answer will have a – 36 in it. Because 12 times 3 equals 36

We can mark off (A), (B) and (C) right away. This leaves us with (D) and (E). Don't be too quick to pick (D). Pi is only 3.14, and that would make the answer a negative number, which is impossible. (9.42 - 36 = -26.58) therefore, the correct answer is **(E) $18\pi - 36$**.

WHAT'S THE QUESTION REALLY ASKING?

The questions are designed to throw you off, so you must CIRCLE what the question is asking. This will help keep you from getting the question wrong.

Example 2-2

If $p + q = 7$ and $r = 11$, what is the average of the variables?
- (A) **5**
- (B) **6**
- (C) **7.5**
- (D) **9**
- (E) **10**

Look at Example 2-2. At first glance, most students would think to add 7 + 11 = 18 and divide by 2 to get the average of 9, which is answer (D). This is a wrong answer choice. If you **circle** all the key elements in the question (p, q and r), we find that we need to divide by 3 instead. The correct answer is **(B) 6.** Always circle what the question is asking.

Another example of how careful one needs to be is shown in Example 2-3.

Example 2-3

How many 8ths is 6/16 – 1/4?
- (A) 1/8
- (B) ¼
- (C) 7/16
- (D) ¾
- (E) 1

Another illustration to show why you need to read carefully can be found in example (2-?) Convert 6/16 to 3/8 and 1/4 to 2/8. 3/8 – 2/8 = 1/8 But 1/8 is NOT the answer. Remember to circle what the question is really asking!

How many 8ths? The correct answer is **(E) 1.**

Try looking at example 2-4. We can easily figure out that x could be equal to three (C). But remember that these questions are designed for you to fall for the "dummy" answer. Always circle what the question is <u>really</u> asking. "How many" are the key words. The correct answer is (A) one - since there is only "one" integer that will make it true. This question was NOT asking you to work it out.

Example 2-4

How many different integers for x will make the following statement to be true?
$$4 < 2x < 8$$
- (A) one
- (B) two
- (C) three
- (D) five
- (E) seven

MAKE NEW DIAGRAMS

"Figure Not Drawn to Scale"—this disclaimer lets the College Board off the hook for drawing an incorrect diagram. When you see these words, it doesn't mean that the figure was scaled down to fit the paper. In reality, it means that the drawing does not correctly reflect the question and if you try to work the problem using that figure, you will probably get it wrong. So, redraw a new figure using the specifications from the question.

Example 2-5

In the following figure, Point P is the center of the circle. If x=120°, what's the value of y? Note: Figure not drawn to scale.

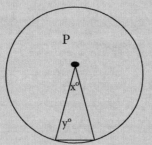
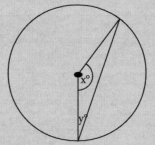

Redraw the figure correctly according to the question.

As you can see, in Example 2-5, the given figure does not accurately represent the proper angle referred to in the question. These figures are often misleading, and it's always best to redraw the diagram to fit the specification outlined in the question. The new picture paints a more accurate representation of the example problem.

DIAGRAMS/CHARTS & DRAWINGS

Don't take the test diagrams/charts at face value. There is probably something wrong with them.

Read the question once, then fix the drawing. (i.e. redraw it correctly, fill in the missing information from the question or make a different diagram to better reflect the question.) Then read the question again to make sure you know what it is really asking.

ADD IN ALL GIVEN INFORMATION

Example 2-6

In the following figure, the circle is tangent to sides WX and YZ of the 12-by-18 rectangle. What is the area of the circle?

(A) 12π (B) 18π (C) 24π (D) 36π (E) 72π

Sometimes the example diagram will leave out vital information that is contained in the question. Assume every drawing (whether to scale or not) is incomplete. They have purposely left out pertinent information in the drawing. Go to the question and get ALL the correct information and put it in the figure. This will help you to answer the question correctly.

Although the question in example 2-6, gives enough information to figure out this problem, the diagram leaves out some essential information. This is why students should always fill in the given information to the diagram in order to help them answer the question correctly. Remember, "tangent" means touching but not intersecting.

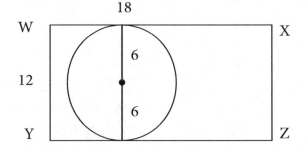

The circle's diameter is 12, and therefore its radius is 6. πr² = 36π Answer **(D)**.

FUN TIP

Sometimes the SAT figure is correct, but it's confusing and difficult to figure out the answer using it. In that case, draw a different diagram that will better reflect what the question is asking and give you a better visual on how to solve the problem.

ALWAYS DRAW A DIAGRAM

Example 2-7

If a square with the area of 36 is inscribed in a circle, what is the area of the circle?

(A) 4π (B) 6π (C) 10π (D) 18π (E) 20π

If there is no diagram in the question—always make one. Especially if the question is confusing or hard to understand, make it clear by drawing it out. Look at Example 2-7.

Make sure you know what "inscribed" means (enclosed inside another shape touching each side.) We need to find the radius of the right triangles by drawing a line through the rectangle. Now use the Pythagorean Theorem to find the length of the diagram, since it is the same as the diameter of the circle.

Diagram A:

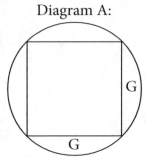

Pythagorean Theorem = a² + b² = c²
$$6^2 + 6^2 = c^2$$
$$36 + 36 = c^2$$
$$c^2 = 72$$
$$c = \sqrt{72}$$

Since the diameter is $\sqrt{72}$, the radius is $\frac{\sqrt{72}}{2}$. Now, to answer the question (what is the area of the circle), use the formula πr^2.

$$\pi r^2 = \pi \left(\frac{\sqrt{72}^2}{2^2}\right) \text{ or } 18\pi \qquad \text{Answer (D)}$$

Diagram B:

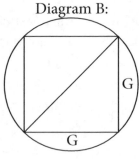

Sometimes a problem doesn't illustrate a specific picture to draw.

Example 2-8

If the sum of all integers from 201 to 300 is subtracted from the sum of all integers from 301 to 400, what would be the difference?

(A) 0 (B) 100 (C) 1,000 (D) 10,000 (E) 100,000

However, it is always a good idea to write out an illustration of the problem, even if it doesn't contain any geometric shapes or figures. See Example 2-8.

If you write out the sum of all integers 201–300 (Group A), it would be 201 + 202 + 203…

If you write out the sum of all integers 301–400 (Group B), it would be 301 + 302 + 303…

Just by looking at it, we notice that every number in Group A is exactly 100 less than the numbers in Group B. Therefore the difference between each number is exactly 100.

$$
\begin{array}{r}
301 + 302 + 303\ldots \\
- \underline{201 - 202 - 203\ldots} \\
100 + 100 + 100\ldots
\end{array}
$$

Between 201–300 and 301–400, there are exactly 100 numbers. Therefore, 100 numbers have a difference of 100, so the correct answer would be 100 x 100—**(D) 10,000.**

ELIMINATE SOME ANSWERS RIGHT AWAY

Most multiple choice questions contain answer choices that are clearly wrong if a student looks at them logically. What's most important is finding the correct answer, not necessarily working out the problem the normal way. If you can eliminate all the wrong answers using logic, you can find the right answer without ever doing a calculation. See Example 2-9.

Example 2-9
Which of the following is divisible by 4 and 7, but not 5?

(A) 25 (B) 32 (C) 45 (D) 56 (E) 65

By understanding basic math terms and principles, you can know that number divisible by 5 will end in a 5 or 0. Therefore, you can eliminate (A) 25, (C) 45 and (E) 65 right off the bat. (B) 32 is clearly not divisible by 7, so the answer is **(D) 56**. No calculations needed!

Example 2-10

The Clay Pottery's old kiln fired 20 cups an hour. They purchased a new model that fired 50 cups an hour. If they ran both machines at the same time, how many minutes would it take to fire a total of 100 cups?

(A) 45   (B) 55   (C) 90   (D) 160 (E) 185

FUN TIP

Always test answer (C) first to save time since answers are in ascending order.

In Example 2-10, instead of doing the long algebra equation, we can simply eliminate the obvious wrong answers. If the machines together fire 70 cups in one hour (60 minutes), we can mark off (A) and (B) because they are too low. Two hours (120 minutes) would result in 140 cups, so we can mark off (D) and (E). **(C)** is the correct answer.

COULD VS. MUST

Two math terms that are important to know:

"Could" means it is a possibility whereas "Must" means it absolutely has to be true.

See example 2-12.

MATH SHORTCUTS (FOR FASTER COMPUTING)

SUBSTITUTE

Sometimes a fast answer can be found by plugging in numbers to help you find the correct answer. See Example 2-11.

Circle the word "four consecutive even integers" and replace them with 2 + 4 + 6 +8.

So, $w + x$ (2 + 4) and $y + z$ (6 +8) would be 6 and 14. Subtract 6 from 14 and the answer is **8** (**B**). Note: (C) and (D) are odd numbers and can be marked off first, since we are dealing strictly with even numbers.

Six, Seven and Eight Work Great!

> **Example 2-11**
>
> If w, x, y and z are four consecutive even integers, and w < x < y < z, then how much smaller is w + x than y + z ?
>
> (A) 6
> (B) 8
> (C) 9
> (D) 13
> (E) 14

Because numbers like 1 or 2 have unique properties, it is always a good idea to use more regular numbers when using substitution. Some good numbers that work every time are 6, 7 and 8. Try this idea in Example in 2-12.

If we use 6 and 8 for the variables, (A), (B), (D) and (E) come out even. **(C)** is correct (6 × 8 + 3 = 51).

A faster to way to answer this type of problem is to know that anytime you add or multiply an even number, it will always turn out even. Just find the answer that adds or subtracts an odd number.
Notice: There is only ONE answer (C) that contained an odd number!

> **Example 2-12**
>
> If x and y are both even integers, to get an odd number, which of the following answer MUST be true?
>
> (A) **x + y**
> (B) **xy**
> (C) **xy + 3**
> (D) **2xy**
> (E) **2x + 2y**

FUN TIP

Adding

Even number added to an even number equals an even number $2 + 2 = 4$

Odd number added to an odd number equals an even number $3 + 3 = 6$

Even number added to an odd number equals an odd number $2 + 3 = 5$

Multiplying

Even number multiplied by an even number equals an even number $2 \times 2 = 4$

Even number multiplied by an odd number equals an even number $2 \times 3 = 6$

Odd number multiplied by an odd number equals an odd number $3 \times 3 = 9$

START SUBSTITUTION FROM THE MIDDLE

Example 2-13

If $4747 = 47(x + 1)$, then x = ?

(A) **10**

(B) **11**

(C) **99**

(D) **100**

(E) **1001**

The College Board puts the answer choices in ascending or descending order. This is important to know because you NEVER have to test five answers. By starting at the middle answer (C), you will know whether you need to go higher or lower and therefore only test one of the remaining answers. If it is right, then pick it -if it is wrong, then the other answer is correct! **This saves time!**

A good way to attack this problem in Example 2-13 would be to plug answer choices into the equation in order to find the one that works. If we start with answer choice (C), we can automatically eliminate 40% of the other choices by figuring out if the correct answer will be larger or smaller than (C). Therefore, $47(99 + 1) = 4700$. By plugging in the middle number, we can immediately mark off (A) and (B), because they would definitely be too small. We can also see that (E) 1001 would be way too large. This gives us **(D) 100** as the correct answer.

FUN TIP

When you are trying to get an equal number-you take a higher percent from the lower number.

CONVERT

Another way to find a quick answer to a math question is to convert. You can turn fractions into decimals. Try this in Example 2-14.

Instead of working a long calculation, convert the 1/4 to 0.25 and 1/3 to 0.33. Make a new diagram to better reflect the question like our example below:

Now we can clearly see that our answer is **(D) .29**.

PERCENTAGE CONVERSION

Always convert percentages to decimals. This will make computation easier and help limit the possibility for error. There is a very simple formula to convert percentages to decimals and vice versa.

> Percent to Decimal = move decimal two places to the left (75% = .75)

> Percent to Fraction = put number over 100 (75% = 75/100)

When using a percentage in an equation, make sure to convert the number into either a fraction or decimal depending on the type of problem. To increase or decrease the percent, make sure the increase or decrease is converted to the same form as the original amount. See Example 2-15.

> ### Example 2-14
> Which of these numbers are between 1/4 and 1/3?
> (A) .14
> (B) .21
> (C) .24
> (D) .29
> (E) .34

> ### Example 2-15
> Paula's famous cinnamon rolls consist of 30 pounds of cream cheese and 5 pounds of butter. What is the minimum number of pounds of butter that she must add into the batter to come up with a batch that is 25% butter?
> (A) Three
> (B) Four
> (C) Five
> (D) Eight
> (E) Ten

First, we need to make sure we label 25% as 25/100. We use a ratio to solve for the answer. Add the parts, 5 + 30, to find the denominator. You could set up the equation as $\frac{x+5}{x+35} = \frac{25}{100}$, and then cross multiply. **(C) Five** is correct.

MONEY CONVERSION

If a question asks you to convert dollars into cents, you would simply multiply by 100. If you are required to convert cents into dollars, simply divide by 100.

Example 2-16

The corner fruit market has clementine oranges on sale for 89 cents per pound. How much, in dollars, would x pounds of oranges cost?

$x + 89$ (B) $89x$ (C) $\frac{89x}{100}$ (D) $\frac{100x}{89}$ (E) $890x$

Look at Example 2-16. This question asks us to convert cents into dollars. Basically if you purchase x pound of oranges, then the cost is $89x$ cents. Since there are 100 pennies in every dollar, you need to divide by 100. So, the answer is $\frac{89x}{100}$ **(C)**.

REDUCE

Example 2-17

$\frac{90}{50} \times \frac{200}{35}$ reduction process equals $\frac{9}{5} \times \frac{40}{7}$

When you have a long equation that needs reducing, don't work it out first and then reduce. You can avoid steps and save time if you **reduce first** before multiplying. See Example 2-17.

Example 2-18

If x = 10, then $\frac{x^2 + 4x}{x}$ =

(A) 14   (B) 20   (C) 80   (D) 140   (E) 174

If we reduce the first fraction by 10 and the second fraction by 5, the equation is much easier to compute. Also keep in mind that you can reduce variables from equations as well. Try this in Example 2-18.

Skip working the long calculation and simply simplify the equation. We can eliminate the "x" from $\frac{x(x+4)}{x}$, which makes it simply $x + 4$. And, if $x = 10$, then $10 + 4 = 14$, **answer (A)**.

CANCEL

Sometimes by canceling first, you can find a quicker answer. See Example 2-19.

The first thing to do is to cancel out every number in sets A and B that is not the same (2, 7/2, 9/4).

Next, knowing what the word "integer" means is very important. (*It can be positive, negative or zero however not a fraction or decimal.*) Look at Roman numeral I ("x is an integer"). We know it is not true since there is a fraction in both sets.

Since Roman numeral I is not the answer, you can cancel all answers that have a Roman "I" in them: (B), (C) and (E).

> ## Example 2-19
>
> A = {3/7, 2, 7/2, 5, 9/4, 9}
> B = {3/7, 9/7, 5, 9}
>
> *If x belongs to both set A and B, which of the following must be true?*
>
> I. x is an integer
> II. $3x$ is an integer
> III. $x = 5$
>
> (A) None
> (B) I Only
> (C) I and II
> (D) III Only
> (E) I, II and III

There is no need to work Roman numeral II ($3x$ is an integer), since Roman II is not left in the answer choices.

Roman III ($x = 5$) is also incorrect since x <u>could</u> also be 3/7 or 9 and the question says MUST be true. So, by canceling all the obvious wrong answers, the correct answer is **(A) None**.

ESTIMATE

Many times you can find an answer by just estimating. Now using this idea, try example 2-20.

Example 2-20

If a square piece of matting with a perimeter of 48" was cut diagonally for a picture frame, what might roughly be the perimeter of the cut mat?

(A) 36   (B) 41   (C) 48   (D) 52   (E) 60

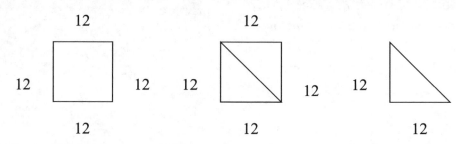

Draw a figure to represent the question. Then draw a diagonal line in the square.

Example 2-21

A strobe light rotates on the disco ball and flashes its light on the DJ every 27 seconds. If the light maintains a constant rate of rotation, approximately how many times will the light flash the DJ every hour?

(A) 27
(B) 62
(C) 125
(D) 2343
(E) 3664

Since we are cutting the square down the middle diagonally, we can automatically mark off (C), (D) and (E) because they are equal to or larger than the total perimeter of 48". We can also mark off (A) because 36" is equal to three straight sides, and anytime you cut something diagonally, that side will be longer than the straight side. So, the answer is **(B) 41**.

Before working out the problem all the way, check to see if the answer can be easily derived through estimation. Mark off any answers that clearly fit outside the realm of possibilities for your estimated answer. Sometimes, only one answer will be even close to the estimation.

Think this through and just estimate to find a quick answer. If a light flashed every 30 seconds, then it would flash twice in a minute. That would be 120 flashes. Since the question said "approximately," we can confidently mark answer **(C)**.

CHECK THE LAST DIGIT

Sometimes by just looking at the last digit of the answer choices, you can find the correct answer or at least eliminate a lot of wrong ones. Try this idea in Example 2-22.

We can find a quick answer by looking at the last digits, so multiply all three numbers $(6 \times 3 \times 1) = \mathbf{18}$.

Example 2-22

Multiply these three numbers: 276, 103 and 61

(A) 1,599,791

(B) 1,630,987

(C) 1,698,212

(D) 1,734,108

(E) 1,815,442

This means the answer will end in an 8, so **(D)** is the correct answer. Notice that only ONE answer ended in an 8. This process also works for division.

In Example 2-23 we can find a quick answer by looking at the last digits (6, 8). Division is opposite of multiplication, so we know that 8 multiplied by an unknown number will end in a 6. Because $8 \times \mathbf{2} = 16$, we need to look for an answer choice that ends in a 2. **(B)** is correct. Again notice that only ONE number ended in a 2.

Example 2-23

Please find the correct answer. $\frac{64896}{208}$

(A) 311 (B) 312 (C) 313 (D) 314 (E) 315

THINK LOGICALLY

Example 2-24

Naomi has saved $30, but she owes her dad, John, 21% of this money and her mother, Lisa, another 39%. After Naomi repays everyone, how much of the $30 will she have leftover?

(A) $12.00
(B) $18.00
(C) $22.00
(D) $23.00
(E) $24.00

In a test like the SAT, where time is very important, being able to save a step or two is invaluable. Sometimes you can save a step by thinking opposite of the question. See Example 2-24.

If you add 21% and 39% and multiply it by $30.00, you would get (B) $18.00—but that is not what the question is asking. It asks how much will be left over, so you have to subtract $18.00 from $30.00, which is (A) $12.00. For a quicker answer, THINK OPPOSITE. Naomi owes 21% and 39% for a total of 60% to her parents. This means that she will keep 40% of the money. So you could just find 40% of $30.00, which is $12.00. It saves a step!

Example 2-25

At the market, Savannah bought nuts for a trail mix that consisted of peanuts at $3 a pound and walnuts at $8 a pound. If the resulting mixture is now worth $5 a pound, how many pounds of the peanuts are needed to make 10 pounds of the nut mix?

(A) 2.5   (B) 3   (C) 3.5   (D) 5   (E) 6

Sometimes you don't even have to work out the problem to find the correct answer. You may only need to look at the question logically. Now using this idea, try example 2-25.

You could work this problem using an algebraic equation, but your goal is to save time by finding the fastest way to work the problem. Let's use logic to answer this question. If the mixtures were even, the cost would be $5.50 a pound. (That is taking the $3 and $8 and adding them together, and then getting the average, which is $5.50.) This is clearly more than $5 a pound, so the mixture is not made up of equal parts peanuts and walnuts. Our ratio is cheaper than $5.50, so there must be more peanuts than walnuts, because peanuts are the cheaper ingredient. If the new nut mix is 10 pounds and if the peanuts are more than half the mixture (more than 5 pounds), then the only answer larger than 5 is (E) 6.

HIDDEN PATTERNS

IMPOSTER ANSWER CHOICES

Most math problems contain wrong answer choices that look similar to the correct answer. The SAT tries to confuse students by writing answer choices that look almost identical. It's important to be vigilant and make sure to select the right answer choice and not an imposter!

(1) Opposites Attract:

Sometimes there will be an imposter answer that is the exact opposite of the correct one. For instance, if the correct answer is 5/7, one of the answer choices may be 7/5. [Example 2-26]

Example 2-26

(A) 1/3 (B) 5/7 (C) 7/5 (D) 1¼ (E) 1½

(2) Double or Nothing:

Sometimes the right answer choice will be double or half the correct answer choice.

Example 2-27

(A) 7 (B) 10 (C) 11 (D) 15 (E) 20

In the Example 2-27 above, (B) and (E) are double or half of one another. If you're not careful, you could accidentally pick the wrong one.

(3) Clone Invasion:

Example 2-28

(A) -4/3 (B) 4/3 (C) 4/9 (D) 1 4/3 (E) 7/3

Very often, multiple answer choices will look like the right answer. These are clones.

Notice that in Example 2-28 4 out of 5 have a four as the numerator. Four out of five have a three as the denominator. If you weren't careful, it would be really easy to fall into The College Board's trap and to pick the wrong answer.

MISSING STEPS

The SAT likes to use answer choices that contain elements of the equation that are correct, but do not answer the question. Very often one of the answer choices will be the number you get after only working one portion of the equation without finishing it. If you didn't follow through with all the steps of the question, you could pick the wrong answer. Read the question carefully and always circle what the question is asking.

Example 2-29

If a = 3b and b = 2, what is the value of 2a?

  (A) 6
  (B) 8
  (C) 10
  (D) 12
  (E) 14

Some of the wrong answer patterns will include: an answer choice that contains the perimeter when the question is looking for area, numbers added they should be multiplied or the product of one or two steps when the question has three steps. Now try and work out Example 2-29.

If you substitute for b, you get: 3 × 2 = 6. You may be tempted to pick 6 as your final answer. However, this is missing a step. Don't forget what the question is asking! Always circle it. The value of $2a$ is 2 × 6, so **(D) 12** is correct.

CONFUSING ORGANIZATION

The SAT has questions that are written purposely to be confusing and out of order. You will have to rearrange the information of the question to the correct order to find the correct answer.

In Example 2-30, the time sequence is out of joint. First, you should rearrange the order to make more sense: Heidi is 12 today. Three years ago, Heidi was half as old as Jeremy will be in five years. How old is Jeremy today?

If Heidi is 12 now, then she was 9 three years ago. This would make Jeremy 18 (2 × 9) in five years. All you need to do is subtract 5 from 18 to get Jeremy's current age. This means that Jeremy is now **(B) 13**.

> ## Example 2-30
> In five years, Jeremy will be twice the age that Heidi was three years ago. Heidi is twelve years old today. How old is Jeremy?
>
> (A) 12 (B) 13 (C) 18 (D) 26 (E) 29

OUT OF ORDER

It is very important to take math terms and translate them into math equations. This can be done by pulling out the information and writing it down and translating it correctly. Then you can see how to work out the equation. [See Example 2-31]

The number of Business Majors, B, at a local liberal arts college is 30 more than twice the number of Music Majors, M.

So the answer is **(E) B = 2M + 30**.

> ## Example 2-31
> The number of Business Majors, B, at a local liberal arts college is 30 more than twice the number of Music Majors, M. What is the best way to express this information?
>   (A) B = 2M x 2(30)
>   (B) 2B = M ÷ 30
>   (C) M = 30 + 2B
>   (D) 2M = 30 – B
>   (E) B = 2M + 30

The number of Business Majors, B, at a local liberal arts college is 30 more than twice the number of M.

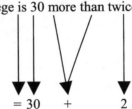

B   = 30 +   2   M

SPECIFIC RULES

GEOMETRY PROBLEMS

Most geometry problems found on the SAT examine a student's critical thinking skills by using basic geometric concepts. However, all the information needed to answer the geometry problems can be found in the question when combined with basic principles. [See Example 2-32]

Example 2-32

In △ XYZ, what is the value of m?

(A) 25°
(B) 35°
(C) 40°
(D) 80°
(E) 100°

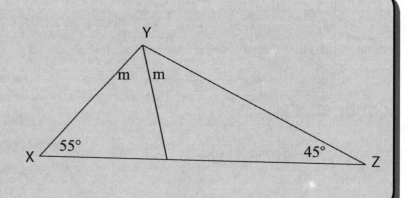

We know that the sum of all three angles of a triangle equals 180 degrees. By adding the two given angles (55 and 45), we get 100. If we subtract this number from 180, we get 80 degrees which is answer (D), but be careful of the SAT traps and look what the question is really asking.

It is NOT asking for the measure of the third angle but what *m* equals. This is half, so **(C) 40** is correct. Notice they were "double or nothing " answer choices.

Even if a problem seems to be missing certain key elements, there is always enough information to solve them with the given information. Now look at Example 2-33.

Remember that all triangles have 180°, and simply by knowing two angles you can find the third angle—just add together the two given angles and subtract from 180. The left-handed triangle's given angle is 80°, so the other two will total 100 degrees. The sum of all the angles that make up A and B equal 150 degrees (100 + 25 + 25). So, if A and B equal 150, then *x* must equal 30 degrees, or answer (C).

Example 2-33

In $\triangle$ ABC, x =

(A) 20°
(B) 25°
(C) 30°
(D) 60°
(E) 80°

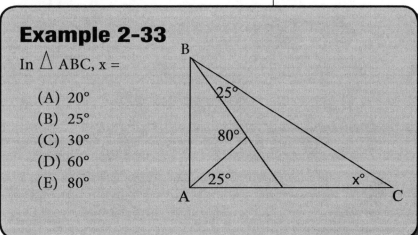

WEIRD SHAPES

The SAT may give you an unusual geometric shape. Look closer—it is probably two regular figures that have been put together. Separate the two figures and use their respective formulas to find the answer. Don't forget about the extra line(s) that put them together—don't add the line(s) twice.

FUN TIP

All Geometry formulas are found on the real test.

When you are looking for a certain length or area, you can find it by subtracting the other lengths or areas of the figure. **The whole is equal to the sum of its parts.** Look at Example in 2-34.

Example 2-34

The area of square WXYZ is 64, and points A, B, C and D are the centers of their own circles. What is the area of the square ABCD?

(A) 4
(B) 8
(C) 16
(D) 32
(E) 40

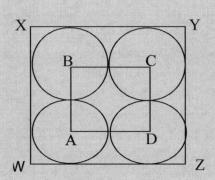

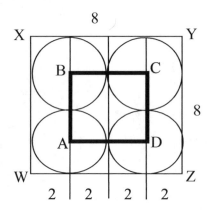

Always write in the information on the diagram.

The question is asking for the area *(l × h)* of the smaller square ABCD. Since points A, B, C and D are all center points of a circle, then the perimeter of square ABCD can be determined by adding the radii of the circles. The area of WXYZ is 64, so the length of one side equals 8. It also equals the combined diameter of two of the circles (or 4 radii), so each radii is equal to 2 (8 = 2 × 4). Draw lines to signify the measurements. One side of square ABCD is 2 radii or 4. To get the answer for the area, we multiply length times height—4 × 4, or **16, answer (C)**.

GEOMETRY FORMULAS TO REMEMBER

Lots of SAT geometry problems deal with finding angles. Keep in mind the angle properties you know about shapes. You can usually find angles by remembering the properties of regular polygons like triangles, squares and quadrilaterals. There are also some very important rules about intersecting lines. Here are some <u>fun</u> angle and line rhymes to help you remember three important rules:

(1) Straighty equals 180

When there is a straight line, the sum of the angles equal 180.
      X and Y are on a straight line, so their sum equals 180

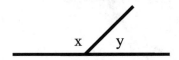

(2) Crossity equals opposity

When there are lines that cross, the opposite angles are equal to each other.

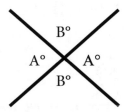
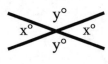

A is equal to A.
B is equal to B.

X is equal to X.
Y is equal to Y.

(3) Leany is in-betweeny

The leaning line is in-between a crossed line and a straight line.

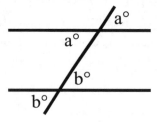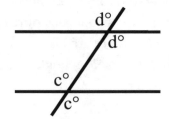

a = b   c = d (opposites)
a = a   b = b   c = c   d = d (crossity lines)

When you put them together, you have a straighty so the leaning line is in between the crossity line and the straighty line.

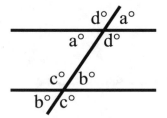

b + c = 180°   a + d = 180°

Example 2-35

In the figure below, RS ∥ TU, what is the value of x + y ?

(A) 45
(B) 90
(C) 120
(D) 180
(E) 260

In Example 2-35 since x is equal to its crossity line, it is also equal to the bottom crossity line. Bring the x down to the bottom. Now x and y are on the same straight line. Straighty equals 180, so

$x + y = 180$, which is **answer (D).**

Example 2-36

In the figure, line A is parallel to line B and both are intersected by lines P and Q. What is the measure of y?

(A) 45
(B) 60
(C) 105
(D) 150
(E) 180

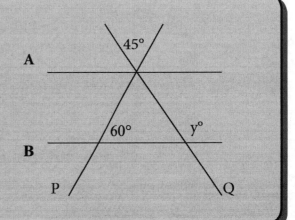

Notice in Example 2-36 that line P intersects lines A and B at the one angle. Also notice that line Q intersects lines B and A at a another angle. Because lines A and B are parallel, these intersections gives us cross lines. (crossity equals opposity) Therefore the angle opposite of the 45 degrees will also be 45 degrees. Now we have two angles of our middle triangle (60, 45) we can find the third angle. The sum of all angles in a triangle equal 180. (180 -60- 45 = 75) After writing the 75 degrees in the right hand triangle, you can find y. Notice the 75 and the y lie on a straight line. (straighty equals 180) All you have to do is subtract the 75 from 180 which equal 105, or answer (C)

TRIANGLE RULES

Example 2-37

In the triangle ABC, the length of BC is twice as much as AB. Which CANNOT be the length of AC?

(A) 8
(B) 10
(C) 12
(D) 15
(E) 18

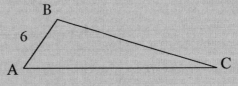

Figure Not Drawn To Scale

An important property of triangles is that the length of one side of a triangle can NEVER be greater or even equal to the total of the lengths of the other two sides. In Example 2-27, if side AB is 6 then BC is 12, 6 + 12 = 18-therefore AC is not equal to (E) and we know that this breaks the rule, so **(E)** is correct. Also, don't be fooled by the diagram because it is NOT drawn to scale.

3–4–5 TRIANGLES

Example 2-38

A policeman drives east on his two-wheeled vehicle 40 feet, then turns north and goes 30 feet. How many feet is he from his starting point?

   (A) 25
   (B) 35
   (C) 50
   (D) 60
   (E) 70

A Pythagorean Triple is a set of whole numbers that can be derived using the Pythagorean Theorem. They are ratios of whole numbers that repeat over and over again in right triangles. Some of these include 3–4–5, 5–12–13 and 7–24–25. If the lengths of two sides of a right triangle are consistent with one of these ratios, the third side will fit the ratio as well. Very often, 3–4–5 triangles will appear in math problems in a disguise. These are right triangles with the Pythagorean Triple of 3:4:5. [See Example 2-38]

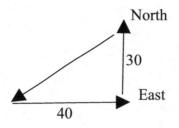

When you make a diagram, you realize that this problem is only presenting a 3–4–5 triangle, this question becomes easy to answer. Learn to recognize this type of problem. They are all based on the Pythagorean Theorem ($a^2 + b^2 = c^2$). Answering this question is simple: east to north is 90 degrees, so the answer is obviously **(C) 50**. This formula is often disguised as 12:16:20, 9:12:15 and 15:20:25.

TRIANGLES WITH CONGRUENT ANGLES

When a triangle contains two equal angles or two equal sides, it is called an isosceles triangle. If a triangle has two congruent angles, then the sides opposite the angles will also be congruent. If a triangle has two congruent sides, the angles opposite the

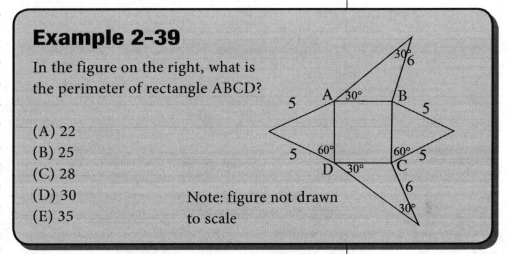

Example 2-39

In the figure on the right, what is the perimeter of rectangle ABCD?

(A) 22
(B) 25
(C) 28
(D) 30
(E) 35

Note: figure not drawn to scale

sides will also be congruent. If a triangle has two angles of 60 degrees, the third angle must also be 60 degrees, and it is an equilateral triangle. All sides of an equilateral triangle are equal to one another.

In Example 2-39 problem is easy to solve using the rules of triangles with congruent angles. The triangles with the sides AD and BC are isosceles triangles because they have two equal sides. The angles opposite the congruent sides are also equal. This means that the opposite angle equals 60 degrees. Because two angles equal 60 degrees, the third angle must also, which means that both triangles are also equilateral triangles. The length of AD is 5, and the length of BC is 5. The triangles with lengths AB and DC have congruent angles, so they are isosceles triangles as well. This means the sides opposite the congruent angles will be equal. Therefore AB is equal to 6, and DC is equal to 6. The perimeter of the rectangle ABCD is the sum of all the sides (5 + 5 + 6 + 6), which is 22 (A).

FUN TIP

The definition of an isosceles triangle is "a triangle with two equal sides." Therefore every equilateral triangle is also an isosceles triangle. However, NOT every isosceles triangle is an equilateral triangle.

XY-PLANE RULES

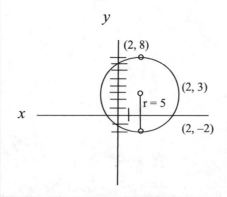

It's very important to be familiar with problems that require you to plot out questions on an *xy*-plane. "X" represents the horizontal line, and "Y" represents the vertical line. Coordinates are plotted out horizontally first and vertically second (*x*, *y*). Remember, to find the slope of a line on a plane, you must find the rise divided by the run or the distance of *y* divided by the distance of *x*. When dealing with these problems, it is almost always a good idea to draw a diagram to help you solve them. [See Example 2-40]

In this case it's much easier to draw a diagram to help you solve this problem. If we make a circle with the center at (2, 3) and the endpoint at (2, –2), we get a circle with the radius of 5. Now it may be tempting to select the answer choice (2, 5) because it includes the radius length. However, we need to chart out five spaces from the center point (2, 3). Therefore, the other side of the diameter will be **E, (2, 8)**.

Example 2-40

In the xy-plane, the center of a circle has the coordinates (2, 3). If one endpoint of a diameter of the circle is (2, –2), what are the coordinates of the other endpoint of this diameter?

  (A) (3, 2)
  (B) (–2, 8)
  (C) (2, 5)
  (D) (3, –2)
  (E) (2, 8)

Sometimes, simple logic can help you find the correct answer to an *xy*-plane problem. Try Example 2-41.

y = 4x - 8

y = 0

0 = 4x -8

8 = 4x

2 = x

Example 2-41

In the xy-plane, the line with equation y = 4x – 8 crosses the x-axis at the point with coordinates (a, b). What is the value of a?

(A) –8

(B) –2

(C) 0

(D) 2

(E) 4

We know that when a slope reaches the *x*-axis, the value of *y* equals zero. In the equation above, only when *x* equals 2 will *y* equal zero. Since *a* equals the value of *x* in the coordinates, then *a* equals 2. The correct answer is **(D) 2**.

STORY PROBLEMS

These question types are generally based on a fictitious life scenario or some theoretical/abstract concept. You need to find the hidden math, pull it out from the story and then set the problem up correctly. Here are the steps to solving this type of equation:

1. Circle all the key elements in the story and write them down next to the story.

2. Transform any math terms into correct math symbols and create an equation that illustrates the problem. (*Knowing math terminology is a MUST.*)

3. Now solve it like a normal math equation.

Here is a story problem that exemplifies a fictitious life scenario in Example 2-42:

Example 2-42

The new hybrid car holds 30 gallons of gas. To fill the car when it is empty, the gas pump delivers g gallons every s seconds. In terms of g and s, how many seconds will it take the pump to fill up the tank?

(A) $\frac{30s}{g}$ (B) $\frac{30g}{s}$ (C) $30gs$ (D) $\frac{g}{30s}$ (E) $\frac{gs}{30}$

To solve this problem, we start by circling the key elements and writing them down (30, *s*, *g*). Then, we transform math terms into symbols and add to the above (30 is total gallon, *g* gallons every *s* seconds). Now we make it a math equation. The gas tank capacity divided by the pump rate is 30/ (g/s) = 30s/g, **answer (A)**.

This is merely a Rate times Time equals Distance problem.

FUN TIP

Did you notice that (A) and (D) were "Opposites" so the answer was probably one of them. Also, the answer could not have 30 next to a "g" since they both represent gallons. This eliminated (B) and (C).

Here is a story problem that exemplifies an abstract concept:

In Example 2-43 to solve this problem: circle key elements (mean, nine, different, consecutive, median) and create a diagram (1, 2, 3, 4, 5, 6, 7, 8, 9). Transform math terms (mean = average, median = middle) and add them to the diagram. Work the problem by adding up all the numbers (45) and to get the mean and divide it by 9—the answer is 5, which is also the median (C).

Example 2-43

If n is the mean of nine different consecutive numbers, what will be the median of those same nine numbers?

(A) One number higher than the mean
(B) One number lower than the mean
(C) The same number
(D) The mode of the numbers
(E) Cannot be determined

Sometimes story problems require you to draw a diagram or picture in order to accurately see how to answer it. Example 2-44 is a great example of a problem that needs a diagram.

When a question asks about tires, wheels or doughnuts—these are round, so you'll obviously think about circles. Draw a picture to help you out. Since the circumference formula is $2\pi r$, then $2\pi(2)$ or 4π.

To answer the question, multiply $6 \times 4\pi$, so **(D) 24π** is correct.

Example 2-44

Mike's unicycle wheel has a radius of 2 feet. How far has he traveled on a straight path if that wheel has made 6 complete turns?

(A) 4π
(B) 12π
(C) 18π
(D) 24π
(E) 30π

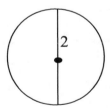

REPEATING PATTERNS

Example 2-45

Josie put one candy cane in a series of eight Christmas stockings. The first piece went into stocking one, the second into stocking two and so on. She does this pattern until 93 candy canes have been dispensed. In which stocking will the 93rd candy cane be placed?

(A) Stocking number three
(B) Stocking number five
(C) Stocking number six
(D) Stocking number seven
(E) Stocking number eight

Example 2-46

Cari's watch runs 5 minutes fast every hour. If her watch is reset at 8 am, what will be the real time when her watch chimes 1 pm on the same day?

(A) 11:00
(B) 11:10
(C) 12:35
(D) 1:05
(E) 2:10

Sometimes a hypothetical scenario will include a repeating pattern of numbers. This can be really simple as long as you look at the question logically. Look at Example 2-45.

Think critically to find the repeating pattern and answer this question quickly. Since there are eight stockings, you can write out a figure like (1, 2, 3, 4, 5, 6, 7, 8). If you divide 93 by 8 you will get 11 5/8. This means that after 11 rotations of filling stockings, stocking number 5 is the last one to receive a candy cane. So, the correct answer is **(B)**.

This hypothetical scenario in Example 2-26 exemplifies a repeating pattern. The best way to solve this problem is by creating a chart to illustrate the scenario. Keep in mind that when a timepiece "runs fast," it is ahead of time; if it "runs slow," it is behind time. Don't just look at the question, or try and work it in your head—start writing down information. In this case, record the correct time (minus 5 minutes) from the watch that is fast.

Right Time	Cari's Watch
8:00	8:00
8:55	9:00
9:50	10:00
10:45	11:00
11:40	12:00
12:35	1:00

(C) 12:35 is the correct answer.

ELIMINATE DON'T SEPARATE RULE

Example 2-47 follows the Eliminate, Don't Separate Rule. This math principle can be summed up in two steps: (1) Eliminate any answers that don't contain ALL the key elements. (2) Don't separate the action/ function needed.

To solve this: circle the key elements in the story problem (x, y, 3). Now you will eliminate the answer choices that do not contain ALL three of these. We can mark off (A) and (B). Now you need an answer that doesn't separate the action needed to work the problem.

> ## Example 2-47
> This Saturday, The Birthday Boom Company has x children divided among y parties. The company wants to purchase T-shirts for each child and have 3 back-up shirts for each party. How many T-shirts will The Birthday Boom Company buy?
>
> (A) $x + 3$ (B) $y + 9x$ (C) $(x \cdot y) + 3$
> (D) $x + 3y$ (E) $\dfrac{(y + 3)}{x}$

Party = y, and they need 3 extra T-shirts for each party. So, you will need $3 \times y$ or $3y$ in the answer. Any answer that separates the two elements can be marked off. Mark off (C) and (E). The correct answer is **(D)**. Notice how you didn't need to solve for how many children were in each party, just how many T-shirts were needed.

MEAN, MODE AND MEDIAN

Terms like mean, mode and median can be very confusing. It is essential for students to learn and understand the definition of these items. They occur frequently on story problems and can be useful to know in your everyday life as well. Here are some acronyms to help you remember what they mean.

Example 2-48

What is the mean of the following five numbers: 10, 14, 22, 30, & 49? To find the mean, we simply add all the numbers together and divide by the total amount of numbers.

10 +14 + 22 + 30 + 49 = 125
125/5 = 25   The mean is 25.

M ath
E quation's
A verage
N umber

Example 2-49

What is the mode of the following set of numbers? {2, 7, 9, 2, 4, 1, 2, 8, 2, 6, 2, 7}
Mode is simply the number that shows up most often. In the case of this problem, that number is 2.

M ost
O ften
D igit
E xposed

M iddle
E xact
D igit
I n-between
A ll
N umbers

Example 2-50

The median is a number that lies exactly in the middle of a set of numbers. When a set has an odd amount of numbers, simply choose the number in the middle.

Set A {980, 1023, 1112, 1476, 1599, 1643, 1755}

For Set A, the median is 1476 because it's in the exact middle by value. Even if the order of numbers were switched around, 1476 would still be the median.

If a set of numbers has an even amount of number, you must average the two numbers in the middle.

Set B {10, 14, 16, 20}

To find the median for Set B, we must take the two middle numbers and divide them by two.

(14 +16)/2 = 15   The median for Set B is 15.

Never again forget the meaning of <u>Mean</u>, <u>Mode</u> and <u>Median</u>! These terms are so important to distinguish from one another. Make learning these a priority.

ROMAN NUMERAL PROBLEMS

Example 2-51

If A is an integer greater than 1 and if $B = A - \frac{1}{A}$, which of the following must be true?

Segment 1: Set apart with Roman numerals $\left\{\begin{array}{l} \text{I. } A > B \\ \text{II. B is a whole number} \\ \text{III. } AB \neq B^2 \end{array}\right.$

Segment 2: Answer choices $\left\{\begin{array}{l} \text{(A) I only} \\ \text{(B) I and II only} \\ \text{(C) III only} \\ \text{(D) I and III only} \\ \text{(E) I, II and III only} \end{array}\right.$

Although the Roman numeral question is usually found in the math section, occasionally it shows up in the Critical Reading section also. Look at the math problem in Example 2-51.

This type of question has two parts: Segment 1 is on top and there are three Roman Numeral numbers; Segment 2 on bottom is set apart by five answer choices, which contain one or more combinations of Roman numerals.

To solve this problem, start by ignoring Segment 2. Then work the problem as usual. When you find the right answer, put a check next to the corresponding number on Segment 1. Then match up Segment 1 (the top) with Segment 2 (the bottom), and you'll have the correct answer.

More than one answer from Segment 1 can be correct. Look to see if the question gives exact or vague details. If vague, work the question from every possible angle.

To answer the above question, let's plug in a number for A (3 will work). So, B = 3 – 1/3 = 2 2/3, so B is 2 2/3.

A is more than B, so mark a check by Roman numeral I (Segment 1).
B is a fraction so put an "X" by Roman numeral II (Segment 1).
AB = 3/1 × 8/3 = 24/3 or 8
B² = 8/3 × 8/3 = 64/9 or 7 1/7
AB ≠ B² is true, so mark a check on Roman numeral III (Segment 1).

Now match up the top with the bottom—Roman numerals I and III is answer **(D)**. Note that (C) could have been eliminated knowing Roman

I is true and (B) and (E) could be eliminated when Roman II was found to be untrue.

In the problem, notice the term "Must be true." It is very important to isolate the terms used in the problems and solve accordingly. [See Example 2-52]

"Must be true" is a clue to eliminating wrong answers. Since there is no way to determine what day they married by this information, we can eliminate Roman numeral III. This means that any answer that contains Roman numeral III can be immediately marked off (B, C and E). We must work this from every possible angle and check out each Roman numeral.

Since there are 12 months in a year and 16 couples, there are obviously duplicates, so put a check by Roman numeral I. Since there are 7 days a week and 16 couples, again, there must be duplicates, so put a check by Roman numeral II. Now, match up the top segment with the bottom segment. The correct answer, I and II, is answer (D).

> ## Example 2-52
>
> At Fossil Lake High School's five-year reunion, students discovered that 16 couples that were high school sweethearts got married in the same year. In this group of 16 couples, which of the following statements must be true?
>
> I.   At least two of the sweetheart couples had a wedding in the same month.
> II. At least two of the sweethearts married on the same day of the week.
> III. At least two of the couples had a Friday wedding.
>
> (A) I only   (B) III only   (C) II and III only
> (D) I and II only   (E) I, II and III

R emember to IGNORE Segment 2
O perate the question from every possible angle
M ark ALL correct answers on Segment 1
A nalyze answers marked
N ow match Segment 1 answers with Segment 2

STRANGE PROBLEMS

The SAT likes to add strange-looking problems to throw you off the track. These are not equations that the teacher taught in your Algebra class the day you were sick—instead, they are simply made up by the SAT test writers. They can be figured out through simple logic. By substituting the given numbers into the strange formula, you can find the right answer. Try Example 2-53.

Example 2-53

Let $S \triangle T = ST + T$ What is the value of $3\triangle4$?

Draw an arrow from each number to the appropriate letter in the problem to help you substitute accurately. To work the above problem, substitute the 3 for the S and the 4 for the T. $3 \times 4 + 4 = \textbf{16}$.

Example 2-54

For all integers n, let $\boxed{n}$ = n + 5 when n is odd, and $\boxed{n}$ = n – 2 when n is even. What is the value of $\boxed{7}$ + $\boxed{4}$?

(A) 4
(B) 6
(C) 11
(D) 14
(E) 15

These types of problems can come in all sorts of shapes and sizes. The College Board is not limited to a certain type of strange problem. Nonetheless, every one of them can be solved through substitution and simple critical thinking. Try Example 2-54.

Substitute each symbol for numbers. When a number is odd (7), use $n + 5$ or $7 + 5 = 12$. When a number is even (4), use $n – 2$ or $4 – 2 = 2$. Therefore, $12 + 2 = \textbf{14 (D)}$.

Sometimes these questions don't even give you a formula to work. You will have to use your reasoning skills to come up with the correct answer.

Example 2-55 is a strange problem with no straightforward equation to figure it out. A, B and C are mysterious letters, but they represent whole numbers between 0 and 9. The far-right column (6, 5, 4) add up to 15. This means you would carry the one to the middle column. This means that A + B + C + 1 will end in a 3.

We can see that a 2 has been carried over in the last column because 2 + 2 = 4. Now in the middle column, if we used 9 + 9 (the most they could be) for A and B, then we would need at least the number 4 for to make 23. This rules out I. Since this is a Roman numeral type question, once we mark off Roman numeral I, we can mark off all answers that contain I—that is, (C) and (E). We know it can't be the number 3, because we needed at least a 4 to make 23. It doesn't matter what the number is—it could be 4, 5, 6, 7, 8 or 9. The question said "could" and not "must." There is no need to go on, because the correct answer is (D).

Example 2-55

In the following addition problem, the digit C could be equal to which of the following?

$$2A6$$
$$B5$$
$$\underline{C4}$$
$$435$$

I.	3
II.	6
III.	8

(A) II only
(B) III only
(C) I and III only
(D) II and III only
(E) I, II and III

NUMBER LINE PROBLEMS

A Number Line has infinite length with the center of 0 and can contain positive and negative numbers. The numbers are separated by evenly spaced tick marks.

Example 2-56

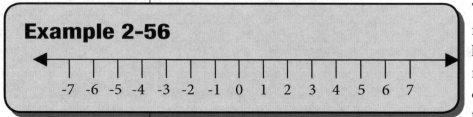

The distance between two numbers is the same as the length of the same two numbers, and the distance can be found by subtracting the number on the left from the one to its right. Example: 2 – 1 = 1. But it is NOT the same distance between two numbers when asked about the number of "positions" between the two numbers. The difference between 2 and 1 is 1, but in this case, count the tick marks, and the positions between will always be ONE less—so, there are 0 number of positions between 2 and 1. [See Example 2-56]

Example 2-57

Jack and Jared replaced their wooden fence posts by spacing them 6 feet apart. How many posts do they need to build a fence 60 feet long?

(A) 7
(B) 8
(C) 9
(D) 10
(E) 11

Sometimes number lines can be found in story problems. In this case, the fictitious scenario is about building a fence. When dealing with questions that mention "fence posts," remember that there are <u>two</u> ends that need to be counted. [See Example 2-57]

Be careful that you don't fall for the wrong answer. Most students would divide 60 by 6 and come up with the answer (D), 10. This is incorrect. Draw a diagram to help you see the problem visually.

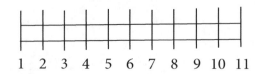

As you can see, there are two ends that must be counted, so the correct answer is **(E) 11**. *When dealing with number line problems, always draw a diagram to help you find the correct answer.*

GRAPHS

Number of Movies Rented in a Month by Seniors at Magnus University

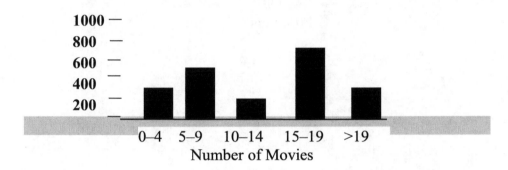

The question in Example 2-58 wants to know the percentage of seniors who rented "at least" 15 movies. (This means you count 15 and every number above it.) The last two bars fall into that category.

Draw a line with your pencil to the left from the top of each column to see what number they each represent. Write the appropriate number above each column. (i.e. 300, 500, 200, 700, 300) We add the last two columns: 700 + 300 = 1000. Since there are a total of 2000 seniors (found by adding all the bars together), then 1000 would be 50%. So, **(D)** is correct.

Example 2-58

In the graph above, what percentage of seniors at Magnus University rent at least 15 movies a month?

(A) 15%
(B) 30%
(C) 40%
(D) 50%
(E) 60%

Quick Reminder:

NEVER work problems in your head. By using your pencil to work it out, you minimize mistakes and clear up your thoughts for the next question.

AVERAGES AND RATIOS

Example 2-59

The average of three numbers is 42. If one of the numbers is 39, what is the sum of the other two numbers?

(A) 3

(B) 87

(C) 104

(D) 129

(E) 168

There is a very simple formula for finding the average of a number. It's called the TAN formula; the total of all the numbers divided by the amount of numbers equals the average.

$$\frac{\textbf{T}\text{otal}}{\textbf{N}\text{umbers}} = \textbf{A}\text{verage}$$

Use the TAN formula: $\frac{\textbf{T}}{\textbf{N}} = \frac{a+b+c}{3} = \textbf{A}\text{verage}$ or $\frac{39+b+c}{3} = 42$

In Example 2-59 first, multiply each side by 3. Now we need the sum of b + c, so subtract 39 from both sides: 39 + b + c = 126. If we subtract 39 from both sides, we get the sum of the other two numbers: Answer **(B)**. As usual, wrong answer choices are there to throw you off. (A) is reached by subtracting 39 from 42; (D) if you didn't finish all the steps; (E) if you multiplied 4 × 42.

Example 2-60

A quadrilateral has four angles that are measured in the ratio 4:3:3:2. What is the measurement of the largest angle?

(A) 45

(B) 60

(C) 100

(D) 120

(E) 360

Ratios are solved in a similar manner. A ratio is a share or portion of the total. A ratio of 4:3 means that one part has four shares for every three shares that the other part has. See Example 2-60.

A quadrilateral is a four-sided polygon with four angles. These four angles add up to 360, since it is really two triangles put together (180 × 2).

Add up all the shares (4 + 3 + 3 + 2) = 12. Take the whole (360) and divide by 12. This means every share is 30 degrees. The smallest angle has 2 shares 2 (2 × 30), the two middle angles have 3 shares (3 × 30) and the largest angle has 2 shares 4 (4 × 30). When we multiply the largest angle: 4 × 30, we get **120 (D)**.

EXPONENTS AND SQUARE ROOTS

When multiplying two exponents with the same base, keep the base the same and ADD the exponents. [See Example 2-61]

> ### Example 2-61
>
> Which of the following is equivalent to $4^3 \times 4^2$?
> (A) 4^5 (B) 4^6 (C) 8^5 (D) 8^6 (E) 16^6

The correct answer is (A) 4^5 ($3 + 2 = 5$). Remember, if the bases are NOT the same, then you figure out each number individually and then multiply.

For example, $3^2 \times 4^3$ ($3 \times 3 = 9$) and ($4 \times 4 \times 4 = 64$), so $9 \times 64 = 576$.

Here's a fun tip that can save you time when it comes to raising five or six to any power. No matter what power you raise a six to, the answer will ALWAYS end in six (and the same for five). [See Example 2-62]

> ### Example 2-62
>
> If $x = 36$, then $x^2 - \sqrt{x}$
> (A) 72   (B) 212   (C) 806   (D) 1290   (E) 1336

When you square 36, the result is 1296. The question asks you to subtract 6, so the answer will end in a zero. Notice there is only one answer that ends in zero—(D), 1290.

Don't forget that square roots can be <u>either</u> positive or negative, and you must assume all possibilities unless the question states otherwise.

> ### Example 2-63
>
> If $a^2 = 81$ and $b^2 = 36$, then what is the difference between the greatest possible value of ($a - b$) and the least possible value of ($a + b$)?
> (A) 0   (B) 6   (C) 9   (D) 22   (E) 30

In Example 2-63 this question is really asking how far apart is it if you to take the largest value of ($a - b$) and the least value of ($a + b$). In terms of square roots, a can equal 9 or –9, and b can equal 6 or –6. So to get the largest possible value ($a - b$), then $9 - (-6)$ is 15. To get the smallest possible value, ($a + b$) then $(-9) + (-6)$ is –15. So, by subtracting these two values, $15 - (-15)$, we get answer (E), 30.

TOP HEAVY vs. BOTTOM HEAVY RULE

Example 2-64

What is approximately the answer for the following equation?

$$\frac{5^2}{4^2} + \frac{5^2}{4^2}$$

(A) –5/4   (B) $\frac{4^3}{5^3}$ (C) 16/25   (D) 95%   (E) 3.125

If a fraction has a numerator (top) larger than the denominator (bottom), the fraction will be larger than one. When fractions are bigger at the denominator (bottom), the fraction will be smaller than one. By recognizing this pattern, you can answer a question faster than using your calculator. [See Example 2-64]

Since the fractions are top heavy, the combined sum will be bigger than one. Only one answer is bigger than one. **(E)** is the correct answer. No calculator needed!

MUST RULE

Example 2-65

If x and y are integers and x ≠ 0 and –x = y, then which of the following statements MUST be true?

(A) $x > y$
(B) $y > x$
(C) $x + y > 0$
(D) $x - y = 0$
(E) $xy < 0$

It's very important to isolate the word "MUST" in SAT problems. In "MUST" equations, students need to find the only scenario that works the same every time. Try Example 2-65.

This question is about numbers but expressed in letters, and it's a bit confusing. Students could start plugging in numbers, like the above example, however this can be a time waster. The answers (A) through (D) COULD be true because x "could" be positive or negative, but that is not what the question is asking. If x and y have opposite signs, then a negative integer times a positive integer is negative—so, only **(E)** is absolutely true.

Example (2-65) illustrates this idea. Questions that involve the word MUST should be operated from every angle. Once a student finds an example that contradicts the

MUST statement, that answer choice is wrong. Mark it off. This question allows for x to be either positive or negative so students should try both. Plug in a number into the equation (-x = y or in other words y = -x) and see the results. For example if a student were to work out answer (A) it would look something like this:

(A) x = 6, y = -6, then 6>-6. Therefore A is true. However if x = -6 and y = 6 then -6>6 is not true. A is wrong.

The "ALLSOME NONE" Rule/ ALL—SOME—NONE

When facing story problems that contain the words All, Some and None, it's important to know this rule: *ALL has SOME; SOME doesn't have ALL; and ALL and SOME don't have NONE.*

By knowing the above definitions, we can answer Example 2-66 logically.

Example 2-66
Some numbers in set A are odd.
If the above expression is true, which of the following is true?
  (A) If a number is odd, it is in set A.
  (B) If a number is even, it is in set A.
  (C) All numbers in set A are odd.
  (D) All numbers in set A are even.
  (E) Not all numbers in set A are even.

(A) This means "ALL" odd numbers. (Some doesn't have ALL.)
   —INCORRECT
(B) This means "ALL" even numbers. (Some doesn't have ALL.)
   —INCORRECT
(C) INCORRECT— (Some doesn't have ALL) *First word, ALL, gives it away.*
(D) INCORRECT— (Some doesn't have ALL) *First word, ALL, gives it away.*
(E) Not ALL also means "SOME"—this is CORRECT.

THE ROAD LESS TRAVELED RULE (TRLTR)

Example 2-67

John drove his new SUV to the border at a constant speed of y miles per hour. How many hours did it take him to travel 600 miles?

(A) $600 - y$ (B) $600y$ (C) $y + 600$ (D) $\dfrac{y}{600}$ (E) $\dfrac{600}{y}$

There are always multiple problems on the SAT that deal with rate and distance. [See Example 2-67]

This is a problem of Rate times Time equals Distance ($R \times T = D$). Pull out the information, write it down and set it up. $(R \times T = D) = [(y) \times T = 600]$

Since we are looking for the hours (Time), divide both sides by y.

$$T = \frac{600}{y} \text{ which is answer (E).}$$

Example 2-68

The Stevens family traveled 300 miles from home to the beach at 50 miles per hour. They came back home at 60 miles per hour. What was the average speed for their roundtrip to the beach?

(A) 54   (B) 54.5   (C) 55   (D) 55.5   (E) 56

There is a quick shortcut for story problems dealing with rate and distance. Every one of these questions can be answered easily with The Road Less Traveled Rule.

When questions ask about traveling, there is a long way and a short way to answer them.

THE LONG WAY:

In Example 2-68 you could make a tally chart and add in all the information: Rate, Time and Distance. Then divide the distance (300 miles) by each rate (50 mph and 60 mph), and you will get the time (6 hours there and 5 hours back). Next, divide the total distance (600 miles) by the total time (11 hours), and you will get the answer **(B) 54.5**.

Many students fall for answer (C). Not because it is the right answer, but because they only average the speeds the Stevens family went, and not the amount of time they spent at the certain speeds of the trip.

THE SHORT WAY:

The **Right** answer is always a **Little** less **Than** the **Rate's** total average: **TRLTR**.

All you had to do is add the rates (50 + 60 = 110), divide in half to get the average (55) and the answer is a little less than 55. The answer is **(B) 54.5**. Since this is the multiple choice section of the test, you don't have to work out the whole problem, just select the right answer. This rule will help you save time and always get it correct.

FUN TIP

The answer will never be the average since you have to factor in time.

STUDENT RESPONSE

T HESE TYPES OF MATH problems do not have any answer choices. Students are required to come up with the correct answers themselves and mark them using a grid-in box. There are no points counted against the overall score for wrong answers.

PICTURE OF ANSWER GRID

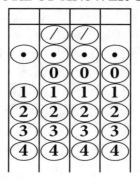

There are several rules for properly filling in the grid-in answer sheet. Pay attention to these tips. If you have the correct answer but bubble the answer sheet incorrectly, it will be counted wrong.

1. Start by writing the correct answer at the top of the box. This will help make sure you grid the numbers in the right spaces.

2. You can start on the left or right side. As long as the number is correct, it doesn't matter where it appears on the grid. However, if a zero is the first number, it has to go in the second box.

3. Mixed numbers (3½) will be read as 31/2 and will be wrong. Convert mixed numbers to improper fractions before gridding in (so, 3½ turns into 7/2).

4. Repeating decimals should fill up all the spaces (.555555… should be bubbled in as .555 and **not** .55).

5. Long decimals should fill the entire grid as well. A number like .719857 should be bubbled in as .719 and **not** .71 (Do not round the last number. You can round up with an answer like .666 to .67 if its a

repeating decimal.).

6. Variables will not be counted as correct.
7. There is no need to reduce fractions if they fit in the four spaces. This saves time!
8. There are no negative answers!
9. There may be more than one answer, so just pick one of them.
10. The grid does not include the dollar sign ($) or percent symbol (%). Convert 100% into 1 50% into 1/2 or .5, and omit the dollar sign if needed.
11. The answer cannot have a square root or pi symbol, so if your final answer includes either of these, it is wrong. Please convert these equations to decimals.

If your answer is negative, a variable or longer than 4 spaces and cannot be reduced (except decimals), your answer is wrong. Go back and work the problem again. Make sure you bubble in the answers darkly and neatly. The machine only grades the bubbled-in answer. Even if you write the correct answer at the top of the grid, if you do not bubble it in, it will be counted as wrong.

The student response section of the SAT can be intimating to some students. There are no clues or hints to the answers as in the multiple choice section. However, all the questions are made with the same patterns and can be figured out logically through reasoning. Even though some of the questions may seem big and scary, keep in mind all the questions are designed to be figured out easily. Try Example 2-69.

Example 2-69

A baby's toy block is marked only with an A and a B on two adjacent sides like the above picture. If the baby throws the block on the floor and it lands with one letter on top, what is the probability that the bottom side does not have a letter on it?

The letters are side-by-side and NOT opposite of each other. There will never be a letter on top and on bottom. The answer is 100% or $\frac{100}{100}$

Since there is not a percentage mark on the grid-in box, and there are only four spaces, the answer MUST be written in as 1 or 1/1 or 6/6.

THINK SMALL LOGIC

Some questions try to trick you into writing out hundreds of numbers to solve them. Every question on the SAT is designed to be answered in less than a minute, so you automatically know that there's going to be a faster way to answer it. There is no need to waste huge amounts of time if you work the questions logically. Try Example 2-70.

Example 2-70

How many three-digit numbers have the hundreds digit equal 5 and the tens digit equal 3?

Chart three spaces like this: 5 3 _ (5 in the hundreds place, 3 in the tens place and a blank for the ones place). The College Board wants to know how many outcomes can be made using this scenario. There are 10 digits (0–9) that could possibly used to fill in this question, so the answer is **10**.

SCARY SCENARIO

The SAT likes to frighten students by taking simple problems and making them appear scary. If you read carefully, you will realize the questions are not as scary as they first appear. Although they make you think you'll have to write out a long equation to solve them, they are probably asking you to solve something much simpler. Always circle what the question is really asking. What is the bottom line?

Example 2-71

If $t^3 > t^2$ and $t^2 > r^3$ and $r^2 < s$ and $t > 0$, what is one possible value for t?

Look at Example 2-71. Although this problem may appear scary, the question is ONLY asking for the possible value of t. It is not asking for r or s. We know that t is greater than 0, and we also know that 1 squared equals 1. All we have to do is plug in a number greater than 1, and it will be correct. You can bubble in any number greater than one that will fit in the four spaces. So 2, or any number above 2 since there is more than one possible answer. Note the answer could not have been a fraction less than one, since a fraction less than one multiplied by itself gets smaller.

SIMPLIFY AND TRY

Sometimes when you approach a complicated problem, the easiest thing to do is simplify the equation and try out different numbers. This can make a scary-looking problem quite simple. [See Example 2-72]

> ### Example 2-72
> Each letter represents a digit that is less than or equal to 3. What three-digit number does ABC represent?
>
> $(A \times 4^3) + (B \times 4^2) + (C \times 4) = 108$

We can start simplifying the equation by working all the multiplication: 64A + 16B + 4C = 108. The next thing we can do is try out different numbers (less than 3, according to the question). Start with the number: 64(1) + 16(1) + 4(1) = 84 (this is 24 short). We know if A is any larger than one, the grand total will be larger than 108, so we've found our first number. Next, we can change the second and third number to 2: 64(1) + 16(2) + 4(2) = 104 (this is still 4 short). If we change the last number to 3, we can get the correct answer: 64(**1**) + 16(**2**) + 4(**3**) = 108 (CORRECT).

You would bubble in **123** as your answer.

THE PARC RULE

Pay Attention — Read Carefully

SAT math questions are designed to throw you off. You MUST read the question carefully and circle all the key words so you don't miss any.

> ### Example 2-73
> If the mean of three <u>different</u> positive numbers is 90, what is the greatest possible value for one of the numbers?

Look at Example 2-73. If the average of 3 numbers is 90, then the total of the three must be 270. You could start with three figures like this: 89, 90, and 91. However, 91 is NOT the greatest possible value. If you think about it, you realize that for one of the numbers to have the "greatest possible value," then the other two numbers must have the two smallest values. This would be 1 and 2. Subtract 1 and 2 from 270 and you get the answer of **267**. This is the answer choice that you would bubble in.

By circling the key words, *different* and *positive*, you know the answer cannot be 269 (two smallest numbers 0 and 1) or 268 (two smallest numbers 1 and 1). That's why it's important to pay attention and read carefully.

FUN TIP

Notice the word "different" was underlined. This can cause you to miss the word "positive" (Zero is not positive.)

TABLE TALK

Example 2-74

The partial table below is John's weekend spending spree for his trip to the city. If his gasoline expenses were the same each day, what were his total expenses for Sunday?

	Food	Gas	
Fri	35		
Sat	41		
Sun	32		
Total			162

The College Board likes to write questions that use a table. When working with tables, it's always important to fill in all important information from the question and redraw the diagram if it's confusing. In Example 2-74 they have given us hint by telling us the gasoline was the same each day. There is usually no need to fill in every box—just enough to find the answer.

The total expenses for Sunday are what we are looking for. We can start by finding the total food costs (35 + 41 + 32), which equals 108.

The answer will be total food (108) + 3 × gas = 162

$$108 + 3g = 162$$
$$\underline{-108 \qquad -108}$$
$$3g = 54$$

Three days of gas cost 54 dollars. 54 divided by 3 = 18 (gasoline each day). Now we can finish Sunday's column: 18 + 32 = **50**. We can bubble in 50 in the grid in answer sheet. Remember, there are no dollar signs on the grid, so don't worry about notating the currency.

WORK BACKWARDS

When your efforts to work a question head-on appear fruitless, sometimes tackling a problem backward will help you find the correct answer.

In Example 2-75 we know that Katie started with x money on Sunday and on Friday she had $1. We also know that every day she had half as much as the day before. Here's how to work this problem backward:

Example 2-75

On Sunday, Katie had a certain amount of money she had saved to spend on her vacation. On each subsequent morning, she had 1/2 the amount of the previous morning. On Friday, five days later, she had $1 left. How much savings money did she begin with?

Make a simple tally chart with the given information.

Sun	Mon	Tues	Wed	Thur	Fri
					1

Since Katie had $1 on Friday, we fill in the last box. Then proceed to fill in Thurs ($2), Wed ($4), Tues ($8), Mon ($16), and Sun ($32). The correct answer is **32**. Bubble in this number into your grid sheet. (Don't bubble in a $ sign.)

Try Example 2-76. If you think backwards, you can easily solve this question by writing down the information and working backwards. Stephanie paid a total of $21.00

Example 2-76

The Red Robin Taxi Company charged Stephanie $3 for the first half-mile, $1.50 for each of the next 4 miles, and $1.00 for each partial or full mile after that. If the total charge for her trip was $21.00, which of the following could have been the total of the mileage that the taxi drove?

(A) 10   (B) 12   (C) 14¾   (D) 16½   (E) 18

Subtract $3.00 (first ½ mile)
Subtract $6.00 (4 miles times $1.50)
That leaves $12.00

Since each additional/partial mile is $1.00, then she must have traveled another 12 miles. Just add up all the miles. (1/2 + 4 + 12) = 16½, or answer **(D)**.

THE P.A.W. LAW

Example 2-77

The 72 oz. wedding punch was blended to put in a fountain. To fill the punch bowl, the caterers added 8 parts strawberry sherbet, 10 parts carbonated water and 6 parts sugar syrup. How many ounces of carbonated water are in the punch?

Parts multiplied by the **A**verage equals the **W**hole. Conversely, the whole divided by its parts equals the average. Question types that contain parts and wholes can be figures out by using this P.A.W. law.

Try Example 2-77. First, circle and ADD all the Parts: 8 + 10 + 6 = 24. Then, take the Whole (72) and divide it by the Parts (24) to get the Average. The Average = 3 ounces for each part.

Last, to find the ounces of the carbonated water, multiply the PARTS (10) times the AVERAGE (3) = WHOLE (30). The correct answer is **30**. Put this number in your bubble grid.

C. C. C.'s PIZZA RULE

Imagine questions involving probability, counting and placement as a pizza company. If you were to order a pizza, there would be three specialty problems available any way you slice it. The key to answering these correctly is the ability to differentiate the types of problems and knowing which formulas to use on each different problem.

There are three main course problems on our menu: Chance, Counting and Combo. To figure out which type of problem you are dealing with, you have to ask IPM questions. You start by circling the key elements of the formula. Then you connect the IPM question to the type of problem you're dealing with. To solve the question, chart out the correct spaces according to the formula.

Main Course (Three types)   IPM (Question to ask yourself)

Chance . . . . Is Probability Mentioned ?
Counting . . . . Important Positions Matter ?
Combo . . . . Irrelevant Placement of Members ?

Side Dish

Circle Key Elements 1st
Connect the Right IPM Question 2nd
Chart Spaces with Correct Formula 3rd

Here's the breakdown of each type of question, the correct formulas and some examples.

Chance Pizza

IPM: Is Probability Mentioned (in the question)?

Probability is always a fraction between 0 and 1.

FORMULA: The probability of an event will be:

$$\frac{\text{Number of desired outcomes (DO)}}{\text{Total number of ALL possible outcomes (TOP)}}$$

For Example 2-78

$$\frac{\text{Desired Outcome}}{\substack{\text{Total Outcomes}\\\text{Possible}}} = \frac{\text{DO}}{\text{TOP}} = \frac{2}{8} = \frac{1}{4}$$

> ## Example 2-78
>
> If a medium 8-slice pizza has only 2 slices with pepperoni on it, what is the probability that someone will pick a pepperoni piece at random?

(1) Circle Key Elements: 8, 2
(2) Connect Right IPM Question (Is Probability Mentioned?) YES
(3) Chart Spaces with Right Formula

MORE CHANCE EXAMPLES:

1. If you toss a penny, what's the probability it will be a head?
A penny has one head and one tail, so the probability will be 1/2.

2. What's the probability of rolling a 6 on a die?
There are six numbers on a die, and only one is a 6, so the probability is 1/6.

3. What's the probability of rolling an even number?
There are six numbers on a die, and three of those (2, 4, 6) are even, so the probability is 3/6 = 1/2.

Independent Probability vs. Dependent Probability

Example 2-79

What's the probability of rolling a 3 on a die and getting tails from your tossed penny?

When doing chance problems, it's important to note the difference between independent and dependent probability. Independent probability deals with combining events that have no effect on each other. [See Example 2-79]

In this example, we see that the number you roll on the die will have no effect on the outcome of the coin toss. They are independent of one another. Rolling a 3 will not make it any more or less likely to flip the penny to tails. In fact, coin tosses are independent of one another. To solve, we multiply both probabilities together.

$$1/6 \text{ x } \frac{1}{2} = 1/12$$

In Example 2-80 each coin toss is still independent of one another, and the probability remains ½. In this case you have to multiply all the independent coin tosses together in order to find the probability of flipping the coin heads three times in a row.

1/2 x 1/2 x 1/2 = 1/8

The result of heads or tails from previous rounds of a coin toss has no relevance on the likelihood of a toss outcome of heads or tails. Every coin toss is independent and has a probability of ½. However, if you're trying to find the likelihood of flipping a coin a certain way, you must multiply the independent variables.

In Example 2-81 this toss is INDEPENDENT of the other tosses, so it is 1/2.

For dependent probability, the number of outcomes is affected by previous actions. Try Example 2-82

There are a total of 30 marbles and 8 of those are orange: 8/30 = 4/15. However, once you take a marble out, there are only 29 left in the bag. This is an example of a dependent probability question. The number of outcomes is affected by a previous part of the problem. Out of 29 total marbles, 10 of those are black. The probability is 10/29.

Example 2-80

What's the probability of tossing a dime three times and having it turn up heads each time?

Example 2-81

The last three times the dime was tossed, it turned up heads. Assuming it is a fair coin, what's the probability that it will turn up heads on this toss?

Example 2-82

There are 10 black, 12 purple and 8 orange marbles in a bag. If you draw out an orange marble and don't put it back, what's the probability of drawing out a black marble on your second draw?

COUNTING PIZZA

Example 2-83

The Triple C Pizza Parlor Menu has 4 soups, 15 pizzas and 5 desserts. How many different meals can be made?

IPM: Important Positions Matter?

In this type of question, order matters.

FORMULA: If a choice can be made in A ways, and after that, if a second choice can be made in B ways, the number of total possibilities is A × B.

For Example 2-83
(1) Circle Key Elements: 4, 15, 5

(2) Connect Right IPM Question: Important Positions Matter? YES! Soup cannot be substituted for pizza or dessert or vice-versa, so order DOES matter!

(3) Chart Spaces with Right Formula
__ × __ × __ =
4 × 15 × 5 = **300**

COUNTING PIZZA EXAMPLES

Example 2-84

How many 3-letter "combinations" can be made from the letters in the word ANCHOVY if no repetition is permitted? If repetition is permitted?

For Example 2-84. Important Positions Matter! Chart your spaces: __ __ __ There are 7 letters to choose from, so in the first space put a 7__ __. We can't repeat the letters, so that leaves 6 choices for the second space, and then 5 choices for the last space (7 6 5). Multiply them: 7 × 6 × 5 = 210. If repetition is allowed, then we have 7 choices for the first space, 7 choices for the second space, and 7 choices for the last space: 7 × 7 × 7 = 343. (*There will never be a question on the test that asks for more than one answer.*)

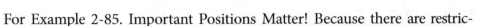

For Example 2-85. Important Positions Matter! Because there are restrictions, we need to deal with them first. We have five different color cards and five spaces. Red can't be on the end (notice there are two ends) so red cannot be in the first or last space (since it is also an end): 4 _ _ _ 3. We've used 2 cards, so that leaves 3 cards to choose from for the second space (4 3 _ _ 3), then 2 cards for the third space (4 3 2 _ 3), and lastly, 1 card for the fourth space: $4 \times 3 \times 2 \times 1 \times 3 = 72$.

Example 2-85

There are 5 cards, each a different color. How many different ways can they be placed in a row if red can't be on the end?

For Example 2-86. Important Positions Matter! We need three digits. 0 to 9 equals 10 different digits, so we'll have 10 choices for the first space, 9 for the second space and 8 for the third space: $10 \times 9 \times 8 = 720$. If we can repeat numbers, we'll have 10 choices for the first space, 10 for the second and 10 for the third space: $10 \times 10 \times 10 = 1000$.

Example 2-86

How many three-digit passwords can you make using the numbers 0 to 9 without using repetitions? Allowing repetitions?

For Example 2-87. Important Positions Matter! The road trip will use 4 roads: one road from Grapevine to Somerville; one road from Somerville to Beach Cove; one road from Beach Cove back through Somerville; and lastly, one road from Somerville back to Grapevine. There are 3 roads to choose from to go to Somerville, and 4 roads to choose from to go to Beach Cove (3 4 _ _). On the way back to Somerville, there are only 3 unused roads to choose from (3 4 3 _), and on the way back to Grapevine, there are only 2 unused roads to pick from (3 4 3 2). So, $3 \times 4 \times 3 \times 2 = 72$.

Example 2-87

There are 3 roads from Grapevine to Somerville, and 4 roads from Somerville to Beach Cove. If Don rides his motorcycle from Grapevine to Beach Cove and back, and passes through Somerville both times and does not go on any road twice, how many different routes for his journey are possible?

FUN TIP

If the question said that the roads could be repeated, then chart out the spaces with 3 4 4 3 because Don has the same amount of roads both ways.

COMBO PIZZA

IPM: Irrelevant Placement of Members?

In this question type, order DOES NOT matter.

FORMULA: Since order doesn't matter, we have to eliminate the number of possibilities where order does matter. We will use the counting method to find the total number of possible arrangements and then divide that by the factorial of the number we are looking for. **A factorial is the product of all integers up to and including a given integer.**

Example 2-88

In how many ways can 4 pizza delivery drivers be chosen from a group of 8 employees?

FACTORIAL EXAMPLE:
$5! = 5 \times 4 \times 3 \times 2 \times 1 = 120.$

For Example 2-88
(1) Circle the Key Elements: 4, 8
(2) Connect Right IPM Question: Irrelevant Placement of Members? The order in which employees are picked does NOT matter. They are in the same group regardless of what order they were chosen in.
(3) Chart Spaces with the Right Formula

<u>8 7 6 5</u>   Counting formula
4 3 2 1   divided by the factorial (4!)

$(8 \times 7 \times 6 \times 5) / (4 \times 3 \times 2 \times 1) = \mathbf{70}$

COMBO PIZZA EXAMPLES

For Example 2-89 irrelevant Placement of Members! The order in which the cards are dealt does not matter. You have the same cards, no matter what order you received them in.

Example 2-89

In a deck of 52 cards, how many different 4-card hands can a dealer make?

<u>52 51 50 49</u>   Counting formula
 4 3 2 1   divided by the factorial (4!)

$52 \times 51 \times 50 \times 49 / 4 \times 3 \times 2 \times 1 = \textbf{270,725}$

For Example 2-90 irrelevant Placement of Members! It doesn't matter if a person is chosen first or last—either way, they're still in the group—so, order needs to be eliminated. Four people will be chosen (__ __ __ __) from the group of 10. There will be 10 choices for the first person, 9 for the second, 8 for the third, & 7 for the fourth ($10 \times 9 \times 8 \times 7 = 5040$). Since it is a Combo problem, and order doesn't matter, we need to eliminate the 5040 (Counting) by dividing by the factorial of the number of people that are being picked (4!). Or, $4 \times 3 \times 2 \times 1 = 24$.

Example 2-90

For a taste test at the mall, 4 people will be chosen at random from a group of 10 people. How many ways can this be done?

<u>10 9 8 7</u> Counting formula
 4 3 2 1 divided by the factorial (4!)

$10 \times 9 \times 8 \times 7 = 5040 / 4 \times 3 \times 2 \times 1 = 24$
$5040 / 24 = \textbf{210}$

Math Completion Process

1. **E**asy is the math. Remember, it's mostly about logic, so LOOK at the problem logically.

2. **A**sking what? <u>Circle</u> what the question is asking!

3. **S**ubstitute (fraction into decimal, good number for a variable)
   Convert (fractions if necessary, geometry figure into two figures)
   Reduce (before multiplying)
   Cancel (figures that are the same)
   Estimate (try not to use your calculator)

4. **Y**ou should eliminate answer choices that you KNOW are wrong.

5. **M**ake a new diagram.
   Draw it correctly or you could get the wrong answer.

6. **A**dd in ALL the information to the diagram.
   The SAT likes to leave out information on the given diagram. Assume it is incomplete and get the missing information from the question.

7. **T**est the answers from the middle.
   Start in the middle at (C); then you'll know whether to go higher or lower since they are in order.

8. **H**idden Patterns now exposed (Clone answers, Double or nothing, Opposites)

E asy math, logical answer
A lways circle what question is asking
S ubstitute, convert, reduce, cancel
Y ou should eliminate obvious wrong answers

M ake new diagrams
A dd in given info
T est answer from the middle
H idden patterns exposed

Write **EASY MATH** at the top of your test page.

FUN TIP

The test is not testing how smart you are in math, but rather your critical thinking skills on a math problem. Learn to SEE the math and not do the math!

PART IV:

THE WRITING SECTION

WRITING SECTION

THE WRITING SECTION WAS added to the SAT in 2005, although it has long been a part of the PSAT/NMSQT. Because of its relative newness, some colleges do not consider this section when evaluating applicants for admittance. They choose to simply count only the Math and Critical Reading sections, pulling scores from a possible 1600 instead of 2400. It's important to check with the colleges of your choice to determine whether they include the Writing section in their evaluation for acceptance and scholarships.

No matter what, you should not ignore this section. With the exception of the essay, the Writing section is an integral part of the PSAT/NMSQT. As long as you're still in your first three years of high school, you should be preparing for the National Merit Competition. There's also a good chance that most schools will eventually count the Writing section in their overall evaluations. Sometimes college admissions officers will read a student's essay from the SAT if they're on the fence about the student's application. This gives them a glimpse of how the student writes and communicates under extreme pressure without editing from teachers or parents.

The essay portion of the Writing section requires you to create a completely original piece of writing during the test. However, the other three parts of the Writing section (Sentence Error, Improving Sentences and Improving Paragraphs) are multiple-choice and require you to recognize basic grammar errors. Just like the other sections of the SAT and PSAT/NMSQT, the Writing section is based on logic and is standardized with standardized answers. Every student should aim to get the highest possible score in all three sections of the test.

Every question can be figured out by using simple logic and reasoning skills. Even the essay portion can be answered in a logical formulaic way. Again, it is learning to decipher the recurring patterns on the test that will help you find

The Writing section was added to the SAT in 2005, although it has long been a part of the PSAT/ NMSQT.

The essay portion of the Writing section requires you to create a completely original piece of writing during the test.

the correct answers. The College Board uses a limited amount of concepts and wrong answer patterns that they duplicate over and over again.

Although you must know the basic rules of English grammar, the key to doing well on the Writing section is discovering the hidden patterns—not necessarily being a grammar genius. So don't fear or forget about the Writing section. It is a necessary evil that is now a part of the SAT. By learning how the test is set up and how answers are derived, you can stop wasting time and start easily identifying the patterns that point you to the correct answer.

> Although you must know the basic rules of English grammar, the key to doing well on the Writing section is discovering the hidden patterns—not necessarily being a grammar genius.

Steps to Writing Success

1. Learn the strategy ACRONYMS*.
2. Know the fundamental grammar rules.
3. Practice writing at least one practice essay per week.
4. Read and understand the rules for this section before taking the real test.
5. Practice taking the Writing section in actual College Board tests.

*The ACRONYMS are designed to help you remember the specific strategies for each section. While you are learning the ACRONYMS, feel free to keep your notes open as you work practice problems. When you take a practice exam, get in the habit of writing the ACRONYM at the top of the paper. During the actual SAT test, you are not allowed to bring in any notes, but you are allowed to write in the booklet. (Do not write on the grid-in paper.) **This is why it's important to memorize the ACRONYMS!**

Format

The Writing section comprises four parts:

- The Essay (SAT only)
- Sentence Error
- Improving Sentences
- Improving Paragraphs

THE ESSAY

THE VERY FIRST SECTION of the SAT is the essay. For many students, the essay incites a grave fear about the SAT from the start. After all, students are given 25 minutes to write an essay on a completely unknown topic. Not to mention this portion will count as 30% of their overall Writing grade. No pressure, right? Fear not. The Essay is just like every other problem on the SAT. It follows a pattern, and if you can accurately imitate this pattern, you can do really well on this portion of the test. Receiving a perfect essay score is not as hard as you may think.

The College Board judges are not looking for perfect papers, but they want to make sure that each paper includes a few key ingredients. The essay topics are usually very broad and general in nature, which gives you an endless amount of information to write on. There is no need to cram information in preparation for it, because you won't know your essay topic until the moment you open the test booklet. That's okay. The test-makers don't expect you to be an expert on the given subject matter. They just want to make sure you can write coherently and accurately develop a point.

The essay will measure your ability to express ideas effectively and evaluate your use of language. The essay should be insightful, persuasive and make logical sense. There are only two types of essays that receive high scores. They follow a simple plan that consistently receives raves from the judges. This section of the book will discuss an overall outline of how an essay should be written for the SAT. You don't need to veer off this guideline and become creative—just stick with what works. Students who have learned to copy this proven guideline have received excellent essay scores.

INGREDIENTS OF A GOOD ESSAY

Essays should contain the four C's of Composition.

There are some basic ingredients that all good essays on the SAT should include. Essays should contain the four C's of Composition. They should Clearly state a thesis; add Competent examples; and be Consistent with the Concepts of the main theme. Essays should also include the four S's of syntax. Every sentence should contain Solid information (no fluff), Sound intelligent (word choice) and have a varied and complex Sentence Structure.

The Four C's of Composition	The Four S's of Syntax
Clear	Solid
Competent	Sound
Consistent Concepts	Sentence Structures

GRADING THE ESSAY

A good essay should express a wide range of experience and knowledge.

Judges will be evaluating essays based on their overall impression of the paper. Judges use the rules of "Standard Written English" when grading the essay. A good essay should express a wide range of experience and knowledge. The judges realize that you only have 25 minutes to develop and write your composition, so they're not looking for perfected papers. They just want to read ones that seem effective and SOUND SMART.

"Standard Written English" is the form of language most widely accepted as being clear and proper. It includes word choice, word order, punctuation, and spelling. Standard English is especially helpful when writing because it maintains a fairly uniform standard of communication which can be understood by all speakers and users of English regardless of differences in dialect, pronunciation, and usage.

They look for good organization, appropriate punctuation, supported examples, solid sentence structure, clear presentation, developed ideas and good vocabulary choices. A few grammar/spelling errors are acceptable, but more than five can start to have a negative impact on the overall score.

The prospective judges will have a college degree and a good understanding of the rules of standard written English. The judges are required to have several years of experience teaching writing at the high school or college level.

Ten days following the test, all essays are scanned into the computer and dispersed to the judges. Each essay will be reviewed by two judges who will grade the paper on a scale of 1 to 6, with 6 being the best possible score. The grades of both judges will be combined to equal the student's overall essay score, with a 12 being a perfect score.

If there is more than a one-point difference between the scores of the two judges, a third judge (Master Judge) will be brought in to make the final decision. The score of the master judge (1 to 6) will be the overriding score and will be doubled for the final score. (The other two scores will be thrown out.)

A score of 0 can be given if the essay is <u>illegible</u>, written in <u>ink</u> or if the essay is <u>off topic</u>.

The judges will read your paper one time through pretty quickly and then grade it immediately for its first impression. Then they will go back through it to make sure you have all the key elements for a great essay. Your score will be then adjusted accordingly. Generally the judges award points to the essay score for every major scoring element the essay contains. They usually spend about thirty seconds to a minute grading each essay.

Generally the judges award points to the essay score for every major scoring element the essay contains.

FIVE SCORING ELEMENTS:

1. Explosive opening/dramatic ending = 1 point
2. This is your overview of your thesis stance. Short philosophical statement that responds to the prompt = 1 point
3. Two to three concrete examples that sound smart, are very detailed and are consistent with your position. = 2–3 points
4. Strong vocabulary words/transition words/bridges = 1 point
5. Five paragraphs = 1 point

Out of a total possible score of 800 points in the writing section, about one-third of the points a student can score comes from the essay. Here is a point conversion chart that approximately transforms the judges' score into the actual points of the scaled score:

Score	Points
12	180
11	160–170
10	150
9	130–140
8	120
7	100–110
6	90
5	70–80
4	60
3	40–50
2	30
1	10–20
0	0

SCORING OVERVIEW

SCORE OF 6: Outstanding mastery. The essay is clear and consistent and develops a point of view on the topic, and it uses correct examples and reasoning to support its position. It's coherent and organized and uses some good vocabulary choices. It staggers sentences and is free of most grammar errors.

SCORE OF 5: Effective and reasonable. Quality may waver occasionally. It does develop a point of view and is well focused. Appropriate vocabulary choices, some variety in sentence structure and basically free of most grammar errors.

SCORE OF 4: Competent and adequate. It will have lulls in quality. It may develop a competent point of view with adequate examples to support the topic. Uses basic vocabulary words and some general sentence structure. It contains some grammar errors.

SCORE OF 3: Lacking and inadequate. Inconsistent point of view and inappropriate examples. Limited in clarity of ideas. Poor vocabulary choices and no variety in sentence structure. Many grammatical errors.

SCORE OF 2: Severely limited. Vague point of view on the topic and uses inappropriate examples to try and support the thesis. Very little organization and no clear focus. Vocabulary is out of place and seriously limited. Sentence structure is problematic. Numerous grammar errors that make it confusing.

SCORE OF 1: Critically lacking. No point of view on the topic. Totally disorganized and has numerous vocabulary errors. Fundamental problems with sentence structure and an unbelievable amount of grammar errors that distort the meaning.

TYPES OF ESSAY TOPICS

The topic question is usually written in a vague, open manner, which gives you a huge range to work with when it comes to writing your papers. You won't be told the essay topic before the test. However, the writers of the SAT consistently use the same types of prompt for every test. Therefore, you can prepare yourself by becoming familiar with the general types of topics. The essay will usually ask you to do one of the following:

- Persuade the Reader
- Solve a Moral Dilemma
- Describe a Plan of Action
- Defend or Challenge a Point of View
- Describe a Turning Point
- Support an Idea

Very often, the essay prompt will present a topic of discussion and ask you to choose one side or the other. All you have to do is pick one side. It doesn't matter which side you pick. The judges aren't supposed to be biased, so it doesn't matter which side of the argument or position you take. You don't even have to agree with the side you chose. You should NOT play both sides of the fence, giving arguments for both opinions. You need to choose one side and develop that side alone. The questions are usually YES or NO, AGREE or DISAGREE. Pick one or the other. Do NOT weigh the pros and cons of both sides.

THE ESSAY STRUCTURE

Once you know your essay topic, the first thing you should do is brainstorm a quick outline.

Once you know your essay topic, the first thing you should do is brainstorm a quick outline. Use a clean spot on back of your booklet to write out your ideas. This will help you organize your thoughts. Make sure the topic question is used in the opening thesis or at the end.

Make the structure of the essay like this:

- A good opening sentence with an attention-getting hook
- Five paragraphs
- Three supporting examples
- Closing sentence that sums up the thesis

Do not spend a lot of time creating the outline. There is no need to write full sentences or Roman numerals—just jot a few words for each of the following: main idea, three detailed supporting examples and a conclusion. Don't spend more than two to three minutes on it.

Now just start writing your essay. Skip lines in between paragraphs to allow for later embellishments, corrections or additions. Also, don't write all the way to the edge. Stop about an inch from the edge to make it easier to change things later.

Write your essay using the **active voice** instead of the passive voice.

State your stance. Don't play both sides of the fence. Make a definitive statement and then give three detailed examples to back up the topic question. Do not write a story! Feel free to write in first person when giving your opinion or describing your personal experience.

Example

The captain flew the airplane.
(ACTIVE VOICE)

The airplane was flown by the captain
(PASSIVE VOICE)

Remember, if you get off topic, it can result in a score of zero, so it is very important to state your thesis or which side you take right away. This lets the judge know you are on topic and it helps to keep you on the right track. Don't be ambiguous or leave any guesswork for the judge to wonder which side you chose or whether the examples actually relate to the topic. You should restate your thesis stance (the side you chose) several times by using your examples to back-up it up.

Write first and rewrite second. Write the body of the essay as fast as you can and then come back and edit it. Practice writing essays in fifteen minutes. Use the other 10 minutes to correct any mistakes and to embellish the paper.

TWO TO THREE VOCABULARY WORDS

SOUND SMART by using two to three good vocabulary words in your paper. When the judge finds a difficult word in your essay, he or she will look it up to make sure it was used appropriately. If so, that generally raises your score. Do not use more than two or three big words. It may count against your score if your essay reads like a thesaurus.

You don't have to learn thousands of words to sound smart, just a handful that you can recycle and reuse over and over again on each paper you write. (See how many ways you can make the same words fit into different practice essays.) The judges are reading the same topic over and over again for 10 days (from 7 am to 10 pm if they so choose). Your goal is to make your paper stand out above the rest. The judges will be amazed that you were able to add great words off the "top of your head."

Your goal is to write the paper first, then go back over it; if you have time, erase two to three lazy words and add in some good vocabulary replacements.

Here are a few examples of vocabulary substitutions:

Wrongdoing → **malfeasance**　　Hard → **painstaking**
Pain → **throes**　　Enemy → **antagonist**
Lucky → **providential**　　Excited → **innervated**

Sound smart by using two to three good vocabulary words in your paper.

Fun → **jollity**

Quiet → **tranquil**

Wonderful → **prodigious**

Joy → **ecstasy**

Success → **triumph**

Scare → **affright**

Loud → **tawdry**

Funny → **risible**

Fast → **posthaste**

Leniency → **laxity**

Make sure to use transition words (bridges) in between paragraphs to help connect your essay together and give it a cohesive flow. Some good bridges are *"Another example," "Next," "Finally," "Sometimes,"* etc. Borrow key words (scope, strengthening, cause/effect) from the Sentence Completion section: *"In addition," "however," "in spite of this," "as a result," "therefore,"* etc.

STAGGER SENTENCE LENGTH

Varying sentence length keeps papers from being boring and monotonous.

Varying sentence length keeps papers from being boring and monotonous. As you write your paper, stagger sentence length. Write a three-word sentence right after a very long sentence. This will help give your essay seem polished and educated. Practice writing a few of them and then try to reuse them over and over again. Adjust them to fit the topic. Here are a few examples:

> I bat 400.
> Children trust me.
> Life is short.
> He still believes.
> God is love.
> Lying ruins friendships.
> Parents know better.
> Tennis owns me.

THE HOOK

This is your reader's first encounter with your writing. Make it good.

This is your reader's first encounter with your writing. Make it good. Start with an anecdote, a shocking statement a relevant quote, pertinent statistics, a preview of your thesis statement, a generalization that will later be proved or some other interesting point. It should grab the reader's attention and give him or her expectations of a great essay. It's like hooking a fish; don't be afraid to take a risk occasionally. Use quotes from books, movies or people. Feel free to change them up to fit your topic.

Quotes and statistics can be **made up** for your essay. However, they must be believable! The judges do not have time to research them to see if they are true and they are not concerned with whether they're factual. They mainly want to know if you can take a topic and develop a good essay using three examples to back up your stance on the topic.

Here are a few hook examples followed by a statement responding to the prompt:

I sat in the rear cage of the police car. Yes, life can take an unexpected turn when you least expect it.

The coughing came first, the gagging in the middle of the night. It was my experience getting pneumonia that taught me that struggles can sometimes bring out the best in people.

"An eye for an eye makes the whole world blind," Ghandi once said. This famous quote can also apply to our lives when we encounter people who spread unfounded rumors about us.

Clarence Darrow once boldly proclaimed, "The first half of your life is ruined by your parents and the second half is ruined by your children," but I disagree—my parents are the greatest influence in my life.

"Harvey Pekar writes autobiographical comic books for grown-ups, but he is rather prone to grumpiness." Yes, I agree that both humor and humanness can exist together.

Suddenly, I realized my legs were gone. This astounding realization is a vivid picture of how one's dreams can appear to be so real, yet so far from the truth.

"David Jones came from humble beginnings and worked his way up to CEO of a successful British retail company and he did so

without telling anyone that he had Parkinson's disease for most of his tenure." I wholeheartedly agree that a disability can not only be a driving force in one's life, but can also be unrecognizable because of the greatness of the person themselves.

The vote was three to three as I sat waiting for my name to be called. And the winner of Survivor **is…Leya! No, how could it be?** Playing the reality show in my own backyard taught me that humility, not superiority, is the key to winning.

I died right there on the operating table. This incident happened when I was twelve and was the motivating factor for me to change my life and finally take my juvenile diabetes seriously.

The first and last sentences of the essay are extremely important since the judges will read the paper one time through quickly and immediately write down their first impression. Make them count!

THREE SUPPORTING EXAMPLES

> **You will need three detailed examples to support your thesis statement.**

You will need three detailed examples to support your thesis statement. Good essay examples could come from literature (books you've read), history, personal experience, current events (recent news topics), observations or research (schoolwork/studies). Here are some good instances of using examples to support a thesis:

FUN TIP

If you are running out of time and torn between three examples and no conclusion or two examples and a conclusion-always opt for a conclusion.

Three examples from my personal life will show you why I've come to this conclusion.

Three occurrences from history and literature will demonstrate why I believe this to be true.

There are three reasons why I strongly believe the way I do.

Three scenarios from our country's past serve as compelling evidence to support this decision.

Be consistent with your thesis stance in every paragraph and restate it differently with each example. Make sure each example is clear, consistent and straightforward. This means you've probably stated your side four to five times before the end of your essay.

Many students spend too much time trying to figure out their three supporting examples. They rack their brains to find specific examples that fit the topic at hand. This is a mistake! What happens if you don't have any specific knowledge about the topic at hand? It does NOT matter! The College Board created the essay portion of the test to evaluate your ability to make a statement and provide supporting examples. It is not testing your knowledge about the particular topic.

This is EXCITING NEWS! The essay <u>does not</u> have to be factual. If you don't have an example, you can simply make it up. Make up all three examples if you have to. If you make them up, don't be hypothetical. Just make sure they are detailed and believable. They must also be consistent with the topic and prove your point. The following two examples are both made up. However, the first one is boring while the second one interesting.

> **Bad Example**: My next example comes from the book, *My Sister's Secret*, where the main character hopes for a new life.

> **Good Example**: My next example comes from Arden Peyton's historical fiction, *My Sister's Secret*, which demonstrates the protagonist's unrelenting desire to hope for a new life.

You can also reuse examples from previous essays that you've written in school or while practicing for this exam. Many high-scoring essays are the result of students just reusing examples they have used before by making them fit the topic subject at hand.

The biggest key to a good essay is to write an essay you've written before.

Practice writing three supporting examples by taking down a list of the personal experiences (vacations, struggles, hardships, work, etc.). Then write a practice essay using the topics found in this book. Do not look at the topic question until you have completed your list. As you write, try to use examples from your list to support the thesis.

This is exciting news! The essay does not have to be factual. If you don't have an example, you can simply make it up.

Practice writing three supporting examples by taking down a list of the personal experiences.

The next time you write an essay, feel free to use the same exact three examples. Continue to recycle and reuse the same examples over and over again. This will help prepare you for the actual essay on the SAT. During the real test, you can then modify these same examples that you've already practiced writing and rewriting <u>many</u> times before. Since the essay doesn't have to be factual, feel free to change names, dates and places to make your examples fit the essay more appropriately.

Before taking the real test, read your old essays and keep the examples in mind. Also, review the books you've read recently, movies you've seen and current or historical events. *Your goal is to use as many of these examples as possible on your actual SAT essay.*

You should be writing at least one essay a week for practice using the given techniques. This will help you learn to reuse examples and vocabulary words in the future despite not knowing the topic question in advance.

TWO ESSAY TYPES

There are two types of essays that get raves:

**Specific Thesis
General Thesis**

There are two types of essays that get raves. Here is a sample topic and the two different types:

Change affects all of us. Write an essay about innovation and how it has affected the world. Give examples to support your position from your studies and observations or personal experience.

(1) Specific Thesis and 3 <u>Different</u> examples

Thesis: The personal computer is a major innovation that has dramatically changed the world. Three examples of how personal computers changed technology in the eighties include…

Examples:
1. Personal computers have changed our personal lives.
2. Personal computers have revolutionized the workplace.
3. Personal computers have united the world globally.

(2) General Thesis and 3 <u>Specific</u> examples

Thesis: Modern technology is constantly changing for the better of mankind. Three technological innovations of the eighties include…

Examples:
1. Personal computers
2. Cell phones
3. Compact discs

You could have 3 personal experiences or an example from history, one from literature and one from a personal experience

TIMING THE ESSAY

You are given 25 minutes to complete the essay section. Use it all up! You don't get any more time.

Take a watch with you and keep track on your own exactly how much time has passed. During the real test, the proctor should give you a five minute warning prior to the end of the allowed time, but if he or she doesn't, you will still be okay with your own watch. Use a chronometer watch or set a watch with a second hand at 12:00 for the essay. This makes it easier to keep track of how much time is left.

FORMATTING THE ESSAY

The following acronym for you to write on your essay pages to help you remember how to format <u>each</u> paragraph. Write it on the outside of the grid lines. This is just a guideline. You may have three personal examples or three from history, literature, etc. Each example should take up about one-third of the page. If you only use two examples, they need to be around a half-page each.

Skip a line at the top before your first paragraph. Then skip a couple of lines between <u>each</u> paragraph. This will give you room later if you think of something that you want to add in. Also, don't write all the way to the edge.

You are given 25 minutes to complete the essay section. Use it all up! You don't get any more time.

Draw a line about a half inch to an inch from the end on the right side. This also gives some leeway if you want to add something to the end. (Words written outside of box do not get scanned to the judges.)

You can use those extra lines to embellish the essay with information (e.g., quotes or statistics) later when you review it. Since the essay is not graded on formatting, skipping lines can help you use this to your advantage. Even though there are two pages to write the essay, a winning essay is usually around 1½ to 1¾ pages long.

Paragraph one:

> **H** ook (Grab their attention)
> **O** verview of your thesis stance (The side you are choosing)
> **T** hree examples (WOW them with your knowledge of three reasons to support the topic)

Paragraph two:

> **P** ersonal or life experience example (Draw from family or friends)
> **O** bservation (How it relates to the topic)
> **W** ord choice (Throw in a good vocabulary word)
> **E** xpound (Make the experience detailed)
> **R** esult (What came about and how does it relate to the topic)

Paragraph three:

> **F** ilm or book example (Remember, this can be true or made up)
> **U** seful outcome (How it relates to the topic)
> **L** anguage choice (Another good vocabulary word here)

Paragraph four:

> **P** ast or present example (This could be from history or a current event)
> **A** pt vocabulary (Recycle and reuse a favorite vocabulary word)
> **P** olish (Make it sound good)

Paragraph five:

E laborate Thesis (Sum it up)
R azzle-dazzle (To get the high score, end with something that will leave a lasting impression)

H
O
T

P
O
W
E
R

F
U
L

P
A
P

E
R

Write the acronym above on the outside of the lines for each paragraph. *When the essay is finished, don't forget to erase the lines you've drawn and the acronym.*

FUN TIP

Use at least one semicolon or colon and a couple of commas in your essay to make your paper LOOK SMART.

PRACTICE ESSAY TOPICS

You can also allow others to rate your essay on a scale of 1 to 6 (6 is the highest).

BELOW IS A SAMPLE of essay topic questions. Use them to practice the writing skills you have learned. DO NOT look at the topic subject in advance. Only read it when you have set your timer for 25 minutes and are ready to start.

Remember, choose one side ONLY and give detailed examples of why you chose that side. (Feel free to make them up if you don't know any.)

You can also allow others to rate your essay on a scale of 1 to 6 (6 is the highest). They can check to see if all the necessary steps are in place to create a good essay by using the guideline "Scoring Elements" (see page 175).

TOPICS

Great gain is often preceded by some loss.
Do you agree or disagree with this viewpoint? Support your position with examples from your personal life and experiences, studies and applications or books you have read.

He who knows nothing, doubts nothing.
Is ignorance truly bliss? Write an essay explaining your belief in this matter. Support your position with examples from your personal life and experiences, studies and applications or books you have read.

Some people believe it is natural to enjoy the hardships of life more than the achievements of life.
Do you agree or disagree with this view? Support your position with examples from your personal life and experiences, studies and applications or books you have read.

"The night has ears."
Do you believe that eavesdropping is appropriate in certain situations? Support your position with examples from your personal life and experiences, studies and applications or books you have read.

If I could create a new holiday, it would be _____
_____, and people would observe it by _____
_____.
Complete the above statement by inventing a new day. In your essay, please explain your choice.

The Bible talks about looking to the ant and learning its ways.
Do you believe that we should be like ants in our work ethic? Support your position with examples from your personal life and experiences, studies and applications or books you have read.

Do you agree or disagree with the notion that a person can be free of all prejudice?
Support your position with examples from your personal life and experiences, studies and applications or books you have read.

Those who rise early will gather wisdom.
Are there advantages to being a morning person versus a night person? Write an essay explaining your position.

If a rich contributor promised $5 million to be used at your school either for sports or for theater and the money could not be divided, which choice would you support?
In an essay, explain the reason for your choice.

Without health, no one can be rich.
Write an essay stating something else we must have to be rich. Use life experiences and ideas that you have developed in your life.

Our world is full of flaws and easily criticized by many. One area which I would like to criticize is _____.

Complete the above statement by choosing a political platform, an organization or a world problem, which in your opinion, deserves to be criticized. In an essay, explain why you chose it.

"He that scatters thorns, let him go barefoot."

Write an essay about spreading rumors and explain the consequences. Support your position with examples from your personal life and experiences, studies and applications or books you have read.

If everyone at your school was cheating on a certain test, would it be okay to cheat in order to remain competitive?

In an essay, explain your position.

Where there is fire and water, anyone can live.

Describe two other things that are essential to life. Support your position with examples from your personal life and experiences, studies and applications or books you have read.

Lying is sometimes the only option if you want to move ahead in life.

Does this statement really describe the way life is? Is this a valid statement or a lie itself? Write an essay using your own personal experiences, observations and studies.

Everyone wants the "The American Dream." For some, it could be religious or personal freedom, economic opportunity or just partaking equally in society.

Write an essay describing "The American Dream." This should not be about your own personal goals, but rather written as if by someone who is not an American.

During the Civil War, children spent 40 hours per week farming. Today, children spend 4 hours per day watching TV.

Do you believe our society is getting lazier or more productive? Support your position with examples from your personal life and experiences, studies and applications or books you have read.

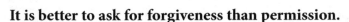

It is better to ask for forgiveness than permission.

Do you agree or disagree with this statement? Support your position with examples from your personal life and experiences, studies and applications or books you have read.

If you want to really know someone, give them authority.

Do you agree or disagree with this saying? Support your position with examples from your personal life and experiences, studies and applications or books you have read.

Many of us live life burdened by old myths instead of being inspired by present facts.

To what degree do you believe this observation of people is accurate? Support your position with examples from your personal life and experiences, studies and applications or books you have read.

"For one to be better, one must first be worse."

Do you agree or disagree with this saying? Support your position with examples from your personal life and experiences, studies and applications or books you have read.

"By the mouth, the body can be ruined."

Do you agree or disagree with this statement? Support your position with examples from your personal life and experiences, studies and applications or books you have read.

"A lie will multiply seven times."

Do you agree or disagree with this statement? Support your position with examples from your personal life and experiences, studies and applications or books you have read.

Revolution causes violence; revelation brings peace.

What does this statement mean? Do you agree or disagree? Support your position with examples from your personal life and experiences, studies and applications or books you have read.

If you live in a glass house, you should not throw stones.
Do you believe that there are times we should judge the actions of others? Support your position with examples from your personal life and experiences, studies and applications or books you have read.

In our great nation, there are things we are proud of and things we are ashamed of.
Write an essay commenting on something that you are either proud of or that you are ashamed of related to our nation.

A person not yet dead is not yet clear of defects.
Do you believe we will ever find perfection in any area of our lives? Support your position with examples from your personal life and experiences, studies and applications or books you have read.

The best things in life are usually free.
Do you agree or disagree with this view? Support your position with examples from your personal life and experiences, studies and applications or books you have read.

Eating a lot will lead to eating a little.
Do believe the obesity in our society is genetic or self-induced? Support your position with examples from your personal life and experiences, studies and applications or books you've read.

Policemen often show courage on a daily basis.
Do you think courage is universal, or is it a rare quality that only some have? Give examples where courage was demonstrated by ordinary people.

Ignorance of the law is no excuse for breaking the law.
Should there ever be any exceptions to this statement? Explain your decision with examples.

"It takes a village to raise a child."
Do you agree or disagree? Support your position with examples from your personal life and experiences, studies and applications or books you have read.

Money is flat, therefore meant to be piled up.

Define the above statement and write an essay about whether you agree or disagree with this statement. Support your position with examples from your personal life and experiences, studies and applications or books you have read.

Just a small change in one area can make a difference.

Select small changes that you know about from your own life's observation or experiences. Write an essay and explain the difference they have made.

Suffering a hardship can build character.

Do you agree or disagree? Develop an essay supporting your view with details, illustrations and life examples.

One never gets a second chance to make a good first impression.

Using examples from your experiences or studies, write an essay that shows how first impressions have made a difference.

In this day and age, the concept of chivalry is dead.

Do you agree or disagree with this statement? Support your position with examples from your personal life and experiences, studies and applications or books you have read.

The United States should require military training for all its citizens.

Do you agree or disagree with this view? Support your position with examples from your personal life and experiences, studies and applications or books you have read.

Are we truly happier when we are getting gifts or giving them?

Explain your thought on this matter. Support your position with examples from your personal life and experiences, studies and applications or books you've read.

Sometimes the end justifies the means.

Do you agree or disagree with this view? Support your position with examples from your personal life and experiences, studies and applications or books you have read.

Television is the product of society rather than our society is a product of television.

Do you agree or disagree with this view? Support your position with examples from your personal life and experiences, studies and applications or books you have read.

Sometimes things are not as they seem.

Do you agree or disagree with this view? Support your position with examples from your personal life and experiences, studies and applications or books you have read.

Everyone has invented something.

Do you agree or disagree with this statement? Support your position with examples from your personal life and experiences, studies and applications or books you have read.

Power is greater than money.

Do you agree or disagree with this viewpoint? Support your position with examples from your personal life and experiences, studies and applications or books you have read.

You can't teach old dogs new tricks.

 Do you agree or disagree with this statement? Support your position with examples from your personal life and experiences, studies and applications or books you have read.

Practice makes perfect only if it is perfect practice.

Do you agree or disagree with this statement? Tell a story where practicing for something paid off or was a waste of time. Use personal experiences or knowledge from your studies.

Not every day is a holiday.

What if everyday was a holiday? If it were, would we be able to maintain life normally or would that be our normal life? Write an essay about how, if you were in charge, you could make every day a holiday and still create a lifestyle that is somewhat normal.

Cheerful company can shorten the journey.
Describe times in your life where friends or family have helped you through a rough time. Support with experiences, illustrations and life examples.

The one who lives longest, sees the most.
If you live to be 100, how would you like the earth to be then? Describe the ideal society where you would live. Give economic, social and spiritual examples for the future.

FUN TIP
Essay examples can come from: Literature, History, Personal Experiences, Current Events, Personal Observations, Research/Schoolwork (True or made-up)

SENTENCE ERROR

To do well on this section, it is very important to know and understand the basics of grammar.

THE SENTENCE ERROR PORTION of the Writing section contains sentences with four underlined portions. If any part of the underlined portion is grammatically incorrect, the sentence has an error, and it's your job to find it. There can only be one error. Usually, around 20% of the sentences have "No Error." When this happens, mark (E) as your answer choice.

To do well on this section, it is very important to know and understand the basics of grammar. Memorize all the grammar rules found in this book as a starting point to prepare or refresh yourself.

BASIC SENTENCE STRUCTURE

Example 3-1

Sue sang.

Before we discuss how to improve sentences or find errors in them, it is important to go over the basic structure of a sentence. A proper one will have one subject and one verb. [See Example 3-1]

Although simple, this sentence is grammatically correct because it contains the two necessary elements. This is also considered an independent clause, because it can stand alone and is proper without adding anything.

Example 3-2

Although she had a sore throat.
And she read the prayer.

A dependent clause is a phrase that modifies the independent clause. These are phrases that begin with either a coordinating conjunction (and, but, for, nor, yet, so) or a subordinating conjunction (although, because, if, since, that, which, until, while, etc.). Please note that coordinating conjunctions are used for clauses with equal emphasis as the independent clause, and subordinating conjunctions are used for phrases that have unequal emphasis to the main clause. [See Example 3-2]

Notice, these dependent clauses cannot stand alone and must be connected to an independent clause like the one in Example 3-1. Sometimes the SAT will include sentences that are merely dependent clauses; these are called fragments. They are improper sentence constructions. Both of these dependent clauses make complete sentences when added to the independent clause. [See Example 3-3]

> ## Example 3-3
> Sue sang although she had a sore throat.
> Sue sang and she read the prayer.

These are both proper sentences because they still only contain one independent clause. Please note: *however, therefore, besides, hence, also, consequently, nevertheless, thus, moreover* and *furthermore* are not proper conjunctions. These cannot join two independent clauses without a proper conjunction added to them. If a sentence has two independent clauses, it is considered a run-on, and it is incorrect.

> ## Example 3-4
> Sue sang, it was the county fair.

Example 3-4 has what is called a comma splice, because it links two independent clauses with only a comma. There are several ways to fix run-on sentences. You could replace the punctuation. Because they are both independent clauses, they can both stand alone, so you could separate them with a period. You can also join two independent clauses with a semicolon. [See Example 3-5]

> ## Example 3-5
> Sue sang. It was the county fair.
> Sue sang; it was the county fair.

Now the sentences are grammatically correct. You could also join the two clauses by making one of them a dependent clause by using a conjunction. [See Example 3-6]

> ## Example 3-6
> It was the county fair, and Sue sang.
> Sue sang because it was the county fair.

Both the sentences above properly turn one of the independent clauses into a dependent clause. The College Board very often will use fragment and run-ons in the Writing section to confuse students. Knowing how to define a proper sentence is essential to knowing how to find the errors in this section.

SENTENCE ERROR PROCESS

To answer these types of questions, first you need to read the whole sentence.

To answer these types of questions, first you need to read the whole sentence. Out of the underlined portions, one of them may contain an error. It's your job to recognize this error. Only the underlined portion can have an error, so the rest of the sentence is always grammatically correct. There will never be more than one error, and there are never spelling errors on the test.

These sentences include a lot of prepositional phases to confuse the subject, but the subject is NEVER in the prepositional phrase. (Memorize all the prepositions from the list on the page 200.) Start by drawing a line through all the prepositional phrases. When you find the subject, circle it and underline its verb to make sure they agree. If they agree, put a check above them to remind you they're correct. Solve the rest of the problem by connecting *each word* in the underlined portion to the word(s) that it should *modify* or *agree with* by drawing *an arrow* to it.

Say each sentence to yourself quietly. Very often, you can pick up errors simply by listening to the sound of the sentence.

Here's a simple acronym to help you remember the steps to finding the error. It's called the ABCDE rule of sentence error.

> A—Always read the entire sentence.
> B—Boot out prepositional phrases.
> C—Circle your subject and underline your verb.
> D—Draw an arrow from each underlined word to its modifier of the word(s) it agrees with.
> E—Error is found (or not found) by completing these steps.

Make sure you know and understand the following grammar rules. These are the most common errors in the Identifying Sentence Error Section.

1. Subject-Verb Agreement

This is the first thing to look for. Circle the subject and underline the verb, then make sure they agree.

- ✔ singular subject = singular verb   plural subject = plural verb
- ✔ subjects joined by <u>and</u> = plural verb
- ✔ subjects joined by or, either, neither, nor, not only, but also = the verb will agree with nearer subject
- ✔ subjects joined by along with, as well as, besides, in addition to, together with = the verb will agree with first subject
- ✔ amounts as subject = singular verb (e.g., "One-hundred dollars is…")
- ✔ indefinite pronouns relating to individuals = singular verb (e.g., anybody, each, everyone, no one, something, amount, anyone, anything, everybody, everything, someone, somebody, either, neither, none, nobody, nothing, one)
- ✔ indefinite words relating to groups = plural verb (e.g., both, few, many, several)
- ✔ some indefinite words require singular or plural verb (e.g., all, any, enough, most, you, who, which, what, that) depending on the noun they modify
- ✔ groups of people require singular verbs (e.g., team, jury, crowd, class, committee)
- ✔ words that look plural but have a singular verb (e.g., physics, news, measles, mathematics)

2. Prepositional Phrase Rule-out

To make sure you have found the correct subject, rule-out the prepositional phrase by <u>lightly</u> drawing a line through it (even if it's an underlined portion). The subject is **NEVER** in the Prepositional Phrase. [See Example 3-7]

Example 3-7

Sub.   V.   Prep. Phrase
The dog ran <u>under the tree</u> to get away.

A prepositional phrase starts with a preposition and ends with a noun or pronoun. Study your prepositions. The most popular prepositions are listed below:

aboard, about, above, across, after, against, along, amid, among, around, at, before, behind, below, beneath, beside, between, beyond, but, by, down, during, except, for, from, in, into, like, near, of, off, on, over, past, since, through, throughout, to, toward, under, underneath, until, unto, up, upon, with, within, without

3. **O**bjective/Subjective Case Problems

Know what is *doing* the action and what is *receiving* the action.

Examples 3-8

Andy kicked <u>him</u>. CORRECT ("him" received the action)
He disagrees with <u>her</u> and <u>me</u>. CORRECT ("her/me" received the action)

<u>She</u> and <u>I</u> think alike. CORRECT ("She/I gives the action)
<u>Whom</u> did he kick? CORRECT ("whom" receives the action)

Subject: I, you, he, she, it, we, they, who (*These pronouns GIVE action.*)
Object: me, you, him, her, it, us, them, whom (*These pronouns RECEIVE action.*)

If any of the pronouns are in the wrong case, that answer choice is wrong. [See Ex. 3-8]

Example 3-9

The constant fighting between my best friend and I started after he accused me of stealing his homework.

In sentences with multiple subjects/ objects, to determine whether "I" or "me" is correct, simply remove the other person and insert "I" or "me" to see which one works.

By removing "my best friend" and inserting "between I" or "between me", it is clear that "me" is the correct answer. [See Example 3-9]

4. **T**ense

Make sure that there is not an unnecessary shift in tense if the action stays the same. A shift in the tense should occur only to show actions at different times.

> regular verb: add -ed for past
> irregular verb: (you should study them for tense)

5. **A**wkward Sentence

By whispering the sentence to yourself, you can often pick up an error because it sounds awkward. If a sentence sounds awkward, find the underlined portion that makes it sound bad. Generally, the more lengthy and wordy a sentence is, the more likely it is wrong.

6. **I**diom

An idiomatic expression is a phrase containing the pairing of a specific verb with a specific preposition that is commonly accepted as correct. [See Example 3-10] There are no specific rules in regards to idioms. It's just how Americans form certain verb/ preposition constructions. Studying idiomatic use of prepositions is recommended, but could take a long time (*English Prepositional Idioms* by Frederick T. Wood is a good reference). If you will read the prompt sentence slowly, you can usually pick out problems with idioms. Here are a few examples of commonly accepted idioms: [See Example 3-11]

In the above sentence, the idiom "at" is used incorrectly. The correct idiom is "eat up."

FUN TIP

If a sentence has a conditional structure (*If he had...then he would have...*), always use the tense = *had + verb...would have + verb.*

Examples 3-10

Define *as*, different *from*, frown *upon*, object *to*, use *as*, accuse *of*, arrive *at*, believe *in*, attribute *to*, abide *by*, according *to*, try *to*, preferable *to*, credit *with*, affinity *with*, argue *with*, catering *to*, intends *to*, superior *to*, ought *to*, partake *of*, different *from*, aim *at*, dispute *over*, agree *to*, agrees *with*

Example 3-11

Margaret watched the bugs eat at the leaves on the plant.

7. **D**iction Problem/Wrong Word

One of the underlined portions of the sentence might contain a word used out of context. Here's a list of the most common ones:

it's (it is)	or	**its** (possessive)
they're (they are)	or	**their** (possessive)
you're (you are)	or	**your** (possessive)
who's (who is)	or	**whose** (possessive)
imminent (about to occur)	or	**eminent** (famous)
among (<u>more</u> than 2 items)	or	**between** (used with 2 items)
accept (to receive)	or	**except** (exclude)

   (*a is before e, so remember you must <u>first</u> receive before you can exclude*

affect (influence)	or	**eff**ect (result)

   (*a is before e, so remember you must have an influence before you get a result)*

real (colloquial)	or	**really** (adverb, means "very")
good (colloquial)	or	**well** (adverb/adjective means "good health")

   Most verbs take well, but linking verbs (to be, five senses: sight, sound, smell, touch, taste) use the adjective "good."

   bad is used after verbs relating to human feelings. ("I feel bad about your accident.")

   badly is used <u>after</u> a verb
   amount (used when something cannot be counted) or **number** (when it is countable)
   fewer (used with a plural verb on things you can count— e.g., months, hours, people)
   less (used with a singular verb and <u>can't</u> be counted—e.g., rain, time, love)

*NOTE: Adjectives are used to modify nouns and adverbs are used to modify verbs or adjectives. Add "ly" to an adjective to make it an adverb. *She ran quickly,* **NOT** *she ran quick.*

☹ These are common misspellings of correct words.

alot	should be spelled	**a lot** (2 words)

(*Remember, 2 words are a lot more than 1 word)*

irregardless	should be spelled	**regardless**
would of	should be spelled	**would have**
could of	should be spelled	**could have**
kinda	should be spelled	**kind of**
sorta	should be spelled	**sort of**

altogether   (entirely/completely) **all together** (everyone together)

8. **W**rong/Faulty Comparison

When comparing items, make sure they are structurally correct. [See Example 3-12]

> **Example 3-12**
>
> Her car was faster than her mother. (INCORRECT)
> Her car was faster than her mother's car. (CORRECT)

When comparing <u>two</u> items, use the suffix **-er** [See Example 3-13]

> **Example 3-13**
>
> Joe is strong**er** than Bill.

When comparing <u>three</u> or more items, use the suffix **-est** [See Example 3-14]

(*Remember, er has <u>two</u> letters and est has <u>three</u> letters.)*

> **Example 3-14**
>
> Between Joe, Bill and Steve, I believe Steve is the strong**est**.

Beware of phrases that double emphasize the comparison like "*more bigger*". The phrase should be either "*more big*" or simply "*bigger*".

9. **O**mitted Words

Sometimes in one of the underlined portions of the sentence there will be a missing word. Read the sentence slowly to catch this error.

10. **R**eview "ING" Verbs

Example 3-15

Many constituents complain <u>about the</u> mud-slinging commercials <u>made by</u> candidates
                                    A   B

<u>being arisen</u> during political campaigns <u>in</u> a voting year. <u>No error</u>
      C   D   E

Incomplete sentences are fragments and make the underlined portion wrong. Make sure each sentence has a subject and a properly conjugated verb. Examine carefully verbs that end in "ing," because this can change a verb into a noun, which sometimes can create a fragment. [See Example 3-15]

By being cautious about any "ing" words found, we can see that (C) is incorrect. It should be "that arise." The word "being" in a verb phrase is almost always wrong because it is usually used as a gerund and not a verb.

11. **D**ouble Negative

Example 3-16

Worrying <u>won't hardly</u> change the future.

There are words with "built in" negatives (scarcely, hardly, never, neither) and you need to watch out for these <u>added</u> negative words that can make them a double negative such as: no, not, can't, don't, isn't, doesn't. [See Example 3-16]

Already Complete Words—These are words that are <u>complete</u> and cannot be considered less or more (e.g., unique, perfect, naked). [See Example 3-17]

Example 3-17

The vase is almost perfect. INCORRECT (It is either perfect or it is not.)

12. **PRO**noun Problems

Pronoun/Antecedent Agreement

Singular antecedents require singular pronouns; plural antecedents require plural pronouns. Use feminine and masculine pronouns for words like "student." [See Example 3-18 and 3-19]

Example 3-18

The average <u>student</u> will take 200 tests during <u>his</u> or <u>her</u> college life.

Example 3-19

Pronouns	Antecedents
I, you, he, she, it, they.	James, Cathy, the bank, people.

James thinks <u>he</u> will be home on time.
Cathy will come later and <u>she</u> will bring the drinks.

Vague Pronoun Reference

The pronoun must clearly show which word it is referring to:

<u>who</u> refers to people
<u>which</u> refers to things and places
<u>where</u> refers to places
<u>that</u> refers to places or things

Change in Person

Example 3-20

If you eat lots of vegetables, one will be very healthy.

If the sentence starts in first person, it cannot properly switch to third or second person in mid-sentence. Watch out for an improper switch. [See Example 3-20]

This sentence contains a switch in persons. It starts in second person ("you") and then switches to third person ("one"). It should read: *If you eat lots of vegetables, you will be very healthy* **or** *If one eats lots of vegetables, he or she will be very healthy.*

13. **B**ut…Also   But Also must follow Not Only

Example 3-21

Susie not only has a job but also goes to school.

If one of these comparative expressions is present in the non-underlined portion, then the other MUST be present also. [See Example 3-21]

14. **L**ogically Parallel

Example 3-22

Bill likes fishing, swimming and to hike. (Not parallel)
Bill likes fishing, swimming and hiking. (Parallel)

If an idea is logically parallel, then it MUST be structurally parallel. [See Example 3-22]

15. **E**ither must be accompanied by Or/Neither must be accompanied by Nor

Example 3-23

She neither wants a dog nor does she have time for one.
Either you will stay or you will go.

Other comparative words that must be joined together are *between/and, both/and, as/as, not so/as, just as/so, more/than, prefer/to, reason/is that, so/that, whether/or* (NOT *whether/or not*). [See Example 3-23]

16. **M**odifier (misplaced or dangling)

A modifier is a phrase that modifies a noun. Modifiers work like adjectives. They can be created by prepositional phrases (preposition + noun), subordinating conjunctions (although, that, when, etc.), appositives (a noun phrase that renames) or participial phrases (verbs with an "ing" or "ed" ending not acting as adjectives).

Example 3-24

My neighbor *in the house next door* loves me. (Prepositional Phrase)
My neighbor *although mean to other kids* loves me. (Sub. Conjunction)
My neighbor, *Mrs. Brown*, loves me. (Appositive)
My neighbor *sitting in the rocking chair* loves me. (Participial Phrase)

As you can see, a modifier directly modifies a specific noun in the sentence. Modifiers must be clear, so they need an obvious antecedent and must be placed right next to it. Otherwise it will be confusing and wrong. [See Example 3-24]

Dangling Modifier—A group of words that modifies something we are unsure of. [See Example 3-25]

Example 3-25

Worrying too much about failure, competitions can be a scary ordeal.

Misplaced Modifier—Modifies the wrong word that it is next to. [See Example 3-26]

Example 3-26

Burning, crackling and popping, the singer stood frozen at the microphone as the wires caught on fire.

The above examples are incorrect because modifying phrases must be placed next to the word(s) they modify. It appears in the example sentences that competitions worry (though they are inanimate) and the singer was burning, crackling and popping (which is inaccurate).

SENTENCE ERROR EXAMPLE

Example 3-27

During the nineties, Paul and Kara <u>were inspired</u>
                                              A
to become <u>a professional life coach</u> <u>after listening</u>
              B   C
to a famous psychologist <u>speak about</u> the struggles
                              D
of today's single mothers.   <u>No error</u>
                                  E

When it's time to practice a sentence error question, read the prompt sentence slowly. Sometimes the right answer just makes common sense. If not, go through the following process to find the (most common) sentence errors. [See Example 3-27]

We can begin to solve this problem using our ABCDE acronym. After reading the entire sentence, we can boot out all the prepositional phrases to find the subject and verb. In this case, Paul and Kara are the subjects and "were" is our verb. The subject and verb do agree, so there is no error there. Next, we can look at the second blank. "A professional life coach" refers to Paul and Kara. Since we know that "Paul and Kara" are plural subjects, we know B is wrong because it is singular. This is our error. We know there can only be one error per sentence, so there is no need to look further. The correct answer is B.

Here is the ACRONYM to help you remember the steps of this process and the most common sentence errors.

A lways read the entire sentence first
B oot out prepositional phrases first (The subject is never in the prepositional phrase)
C ircle the subject—underline the verb to see if they agree
D raw an arrow from each underlined word to the word it modifies/agrees with
E rror now found (if any)

S ubject-Verb agreement—Circle the subject and underline the verb, then make sure they agree.

P repositional Phrase rule-out—Draw a line through the prepositional phrase to find the subject.

O bjective/Subjective Case—See if they are in the correct case (subjective/objective)

T ense—Check ALL the verbs and make sure they are in the <u>SAME</u> tense.

A wkward—Read the sentence slowly. If the sentence sounds awkward, find the error in the underlined portion.

I diom—Check to make sure the idiomatic use of prepositions is appropriate.

D iction Problem—See if the underlined word is spelled another way or used in a different fashion than normal. *Look for tricky wrong word spellings/meanings.*

W rong/Faulty Comparison—Proper suffixes and structurally correct sentences with comparisons

O mitted Word—Read prompt sentence slowly for missing word in the underlined portions.

R eview "ING" Words—If underlined portion makes an incomplete sentence, it is wrong.

D ouble Negative—Watch out for words that are already negative and may have a *no, not,*   *can't or don't* added to them. (Keep *complete* words *complete*)

PRO noun Problem—Pronouns and antecedents must agree/ clear reference to pronoun reference

B ut…Also—If there is one of these comparatives, make sure the other one is in the sentence.

L ogically Parallel—Make sure the ideas are structurally parallel.

E ither…Or—Neither…Nor

M odifier—Check to see if there are any dangling or misplaced modifiers.

Write **ABCDE SPOT & AID WORD PROBLEM** at the top of the test page.

IMPROVING SENTENCES

If there is a problem with the sentence, it is ONLY found in the underlined portion.

THE QUESTIONS IN THIS section contain a sentence with all of it (or a portion of it) underlined. If there is a problem with the sentence, it is ONLY found in the underlined portion. You will need to find the best restatement of that portion. If there is no problem, then answer (A) is correct. Answer (A) is the unchanged sentence. *To save time, don't read answer* (A). Around 20% of the sentences are error-free.

The correct answer must be BOTH grammatically correct <u>AND</u> the best **RESTATEMENT.** If there is an error in the underlined portion, it will be a grammar error (there won't be any spelling errors). Answer (A) is only correct if there are no errors.

IMPROVING SENTENCES PROCESS

First, you will want to read the complete prompt sentence, not just the underlined section.

First, you will want to read the complete prompt sentence, not just the underlined section. Then you can concentrate on the underlined part to see if it has broken any of the grammar rules.

Circle the subject and underline the verb to make sure they agree <u>after</u> you have drawn a line through each prepositional phrase. This ensures finding the right subject.

Next, find what is wrong (if anything) and mark off ALL answer choices that have the same problem. You can usually mark off two to three answers right off the bat this way. Usually, you don't have to read the entire answer choice to know if it repeats the same problem.

Finally, look at the beginning of each sentence in the answer choices. Decide which word the correct answer will start with. You can usually mark off two to three answers this way as well. Remember, you are looking for the most concise answer with the best RESTATEMENT.

Eliminate wrong answers first and then insert remaining answer choices into the sentence to find the correct answer. Make sure you understand the parts of speech in a sentence. Review grammar rules if necessary.

The correct answer tends to be either the longest or the shortest choice. Since you are looking for the most concise and best restatement, the answer is usually the <u>shortest</u> one. If the sentence is missing key elements, it is probably the longest answer. **Zero in on these two answer choices first.**

The right answer will be concise, grammatically correct and make the most sense.

Here are the most common problems in this section:

1. **R**eview Fragment or Run-On Sentences
    If the answer choice makes an incomplete sentence, then it is a fragment and it is wrong.
    If two complete sentences are spliced together, they need to either be separated by a period, conjunction, semicolon or the word "because."

2. **E**xtremely Awkward
    While reading the answer choices, if any of them sound awkward, then they are probably wrong. Whisper the sentence to yourself because this can very often help you pick up an awkward-sounding part of the sentence.

3. **S**emicolon, Comma Splice and Punctuation
    Know the rules of punctuation and check to see if the answer choices have broken any of the rules.

The correct answer is usually just the shortest one!

semicolon—used with two independent clauses that are closely related; for setting apart parts of a list.

commas—used after a pause; after four or more intro words; precedes an *and, or, for, nor, so, yet*; in a compound sentence; to set off appositives.

quotation marks—periods and commas go inside of quotation marks while question marks, exclamation points, colons and semicolons go inside only if they are part of the quoted material.

Capitalize what is appropriate:

First word of sentence or direct quote; proper nouns; names of ships, aircrafts, trains, deities, geological periods, astronomical bodies, personifications, historical periods, associations and government offices; first and last word of a title; newspaper and magazine titles; radio and TV call letters; regions; specific military branches; political groups; nationalities; days; holidays; months; and trademarks.

Italicize the bigger item—Put the smaller item in quotations

Book (*Jane Eyre*)   Chapter of book ("My Day")
Movie (*Spider-Man*)   TV Show ("Jeopardy!")
Newspaper (*New York Times*) Story ("My Summer")
Magazines (*Good Housekeeping*) Poem ("Stopping By Woods on a Snowy Evening")

4. **T**oo Wordy

The right answer is a concise restatement without using too many words. If you find an answer choice that's too wordy, it's probably wrong. The shortest answers are often the best, unless the underlined portion left some important information out.

5. **A**ppositive
This is a part of the sentence that is nonessential and needs a comma to set it off. If left out, the basic meaning of the sentence would stay intact. [See Example 3-28]

Example 3-28

Mark Twain's *Huckleberry Finn*, <u>expanded and revised</u>, is an excellent book.

6. **T**roubling Pronoun-Antecedent
Follow previous rules for any pronoun problems.

7. **E**xchanged Words—a similar word will be in place of the right word. [See Example 3-29]

Example 3-29

The victim gave a *prescription*. (INCORRECT)
The victim gave a *description*. (CORRECT)

8. **M**odifier—Dangling or Misplaced
A <u>dangling</u> modifier is a word or group of words that modifies something we are unsure of because that something is missing.
A <u>misplaced</u> modifier modifies the wrong word or words by being too close to them.

9. **E**xtra, Confusing, Contradicting and Irrelevant
Follow previous rules to eliminate any of these in the underlined portions of the wrong answer choices.

10. **N**eeds a Conjunction/Preposition
For the answer to make sense, it may need a conjunction (*and, or, but, nor, for, so, yet*) or a connecting preposition.

11. **T**otally Restates

The correct answer choice will **always restate** the underlined portion of the prompt sentence and will be concise, non-awkward and make sense.

Example 3-30

Like most new residents, <u>the city's twisting roads confused the Davis family</u> for the first week.

(A) <u>the city's twisting roads</u> confused the Davis family
(B) <u>the twisting roads</u> of the city confusing the Davis family
(C) <u>the Davis family</u> was confused by the city's twisting roads
(D) <u>the Davis family</u>, who found the city's twisting roads confusing
(E) <u>there were twisting roads</u> in the city which confused the Davis family

Now using these grammar rules, we can look at Example 3-30. Remember that the correct answer will fix whatever problem the original sentence contained and properly restate the same idea of the original sentence. (*Remember that if the prompt sentence is correct, then the first answer (A) is unchanged and will be the right answer.*)

Notice the pattern of the answer choices. Three of them start off with "twisting roads", and two with "Davis family". Obviously we'll be able to mark-off two to three right away once we know what the sentence will start with. What's the error in this sentence? If we look at the word "residents", we see the problem is a misplaced modifier. Knowing that we are trying to modify residents, we can mark off (A), (B) and (E) right off the bat without even reading them. Between the two left, **(C)** is the most concise, makes the most sense and is the shorter of the two answers.

Here is an acronym to help you remember the types of errors that most commonly occur in the improving sentences section:

R eview whether it's a fragment/run-on
E xtremely awkward
S emicolon/punctuation
T oo wordy—look at shortest answers first
A ppositive
T roubling pronoun-antecedent
E xchanged word
M odifier (dangling, misplaced)
E xtra, confusing, contradictory, irrelevant
N eeds conjunction
T otally restates

Write **RESTATEMENT** at the top of your test page.

IMPROVING PARAGRAPHS

Improving Paragraphs is nothing more than a combination of the Passage-Based Reading (paragraph skimming) and the Improving Sentence (fixing punctuation) sections.

THIS SECTION CONSISTS OF a short passage with numbered sentences. The questions will ask about the relationship between sentences or the possibility of combining them. Improving Paragraphs is nothing more than a combination of the Passage-Based Reading (paragraph skimming) and the Improving Sentence (fixing punctuation) sections.

You will mainly need to **REVISE** any sentences that are poorly written or grammatically incorrect. If an answer choice introduces a new idea, it is WRONG! The best answer will restate the information of the first sentence better.

Remember, they are NOT asking you for your opinion, so every answer can be found in the text. The test is not subjective. There is ONLY one correct answer. Use deductive reasoning if the author implies the answer. You will have to draw an inference from the author's hints.

Since this section is similar to the Passage-Based Reading portion, you should treat it the same. Don't read the passage since the line citation sentence is almost always reproduced in the question. Skim the passage, circle the citations (if not reproduced in the question) and save the overall passage questions until the end. To get a good idea of each paragraph, read the first and last sentences.

Also, just like in the Improving Sentences section, watch out for the same wrong grammatical patterns. Review all of the grammar rules.

Some wrong patterns can be: fragments, semicolons, appositives, pronoun agreement, incorrect conjunctions, wrong verb tense, modifier problems, parallel problems or extra words.

Improving Paragraph Example:

(1) It was early in the morning when I arrived for my unearthing. (2) I was in India starting a new adventure. (3) I was to stay in a hut on the edge of the Ganges River, about 150 miles southwest of down town Mumbai. (4) I was to stay there for the rest of the summer, acting as a vagabond with no place truly to call home.

(5) It was a particularly hot for that time of the year, the sun had set hours before but it felt as though it was still the middle of the day. (6) Sweat rolled down my face as I walked out from the airport's terminal. (7) I passed the baggage claim with a sigh of relief, no need to wait I thought, just me and my carry on backpack. (8) It was pure joy. (9) It felt great knowing my backpack was the only thing I owned. (10) It was the only thing I had to take care of, well other than myself.

(11) The streets were crowded with taxi cabdrivers. (12) Each was clamoring for my business. (13) "What hotel you going to 'Sir'," they would ask me. (14) I just smiled and waved them on. (15) I preferred to walk. (16) Satisfaction filled my soul, not sure where I was going, or who I'd meet. (17) I was there to find myself.

FOUR QUESTION TYPES

Below are the four question types that can be found on the Improving Paragraphs Section. Keep in mind that all the previous rules from the Critical Reading section still apply.

> 1. **INSERTION QUESTIONS**
> 2. **AUTHOR'S THOUGHTS**
> 3. **REVISION QUESTIONS**
> 4. **AUTHOR'S ARGUMENTS**

INSERTION QUESTIONS

Where do we insert a new sentence? These question types ask about sentences that can be inserted at any given place in the paragraph. First READ the first and last lines of each the paragraph to <u>find the theme of that portion</u>. Then, look at the themes of each answer choice. Only one answer choice will appropriately match the paragraph's theme and fit logically. The answer choice that fits in context of the passage and strengthens the passage's meaning is the correct answer.

Only add in a sentence if the information in it doesn't contradict the paragraph, contain additional information, seem irrelevant or sound obscure.

Only add in a sentence if the information in it doesn't contradict the paragraph, contain additional information, seem irrelevant or sound obscure. Only delete a sentence if the information doesn't agree with the rest of the paragraph by containing one of the above hidden patterns. When deciding whether you need to add or delete a sentence in the passage, <u>always read from the line before and after</u> to make sure the sentence fits with the context of the paragraph.

Remember to eliminate wrong answer choices- those that have been COATed with the hidden tricks.

> (7) *I passed the baggage claim with a sigh of relief, no need to wait I thought, just me and my carry on backpack. (8) It was pure joy. (9) It felt great knowing my backpack was the only thing I owned.*

Example 3-31

In context, which words should be inserted after "pure joy" in sentence 8 to complete the author's thought?

   (A) to be off the plane
   (B) to be so free
   (C) to ignore the taxi drivers
   (D) to walk around India
   (E) to be homeless

Example 3-31 is an example of an "insertion" question. To find the answer, you must read at least the line before and after sentence (8). Don't be fooled by "baggage claim" in line (7) and pick answer (A). This is a trap. If you read the lines after (8), it's easy to see that the author is talking about not being tied to anything material and therefore (B) is the correct answer. (It's also the shortest answer.)

AUTHOR'S THOUGHTS

What is the author thinking? These question types ask about the author's strategy. Usually you are given five answer choices that illustrate an idea about the passage. You are then asked which of the five choices was used in the passage **OR** which of the five was not used in the passage. You should be able to find at least one clear-cut example of the correct answer in the paragraph. Search until you find either the one that is there or the four that are not there. *MARK OUT wrong answers when you find them. Try working out Example 3-32.*

Example 3-32

Why did the author choose to travel like a vagabond?
   (A) He was tired of the rat race of everyday life
   (B) He sympathized with the people of Mumbai who owned very little
   (C) Walking all around the world was a passion of his
   (D) This was his last chance of happiness
   (E) He desired deep discovery of his inner self

   (1) It was early in the morning when I arrived for my unearthing…
   (17) I was there to find myself.

Now, the problem with most of the answer choices for this question is that they add too much information. Answer choices (A), (B), (C) and (D) all contain information that is not explicitly implied in the passage. If we look at the first and last lines of the passage, we can find the author's thoughts. The author is traveling like a vagabond (unearthing means "finding") because he wants to "find himself." Answer **(E)** is correct.

REVISION QUESTIONS

Example 3-33

Which of the following would is the best way to revise the underlined portions of sentences 9 and 10 (reproduced below)?

(9) It felt great knowing my backpack was the <u>only thing I owned. (10) It was the only thing I had to take care of,</u> well other than myself.

(A) leave as is

(B) only thing I owned and it was the only thing I had to take care of

(C) being that it was the only thing I owned it was also the only thing I had to take care of

(D) only thing I owned and all I had to care for

(E) being my only thing it was all I had to take care of

How do you best revise the sentence? This question type asks how a sentence or two can be written better. It may ask you to improve, rephrase, delete or combine sentences. As you read the sentence, consider any awkward wording or any unclear phrasing. If there are two sentences, find the relationship between the two. A clear-cut relationship should be obvious. Be sure to read the sentences carefully. Try working out Example 3-33.

By looking at the excerpt, we notice a clear relationship between the two sentences. They both refer to the narrator's backpack as the "only thing." We notice there is some redundancy in the two sentences, so the best way to revise the sentences above will be to eliminate the redundancy. Answer choice (D) does the best job at this in a clear and concise manner.

AUTHOR'S ARGUMENTS

What's the strongest argument? These question types are about the main idea of the passage. Sometimes questions suggest a hypothetical paragraph that could make the author's position/argument stronger. In the answer choices, there will be one <u>obvious</u> answer that perfectly fits the position of the passage. Refer to first and last lines of the passage to help find the correct answer. Use this information to answer Example 3-34.

Notice how most of the answer choices are opinionated and break the SON rule. Words like "only" and "natives/imposed upon" prove those answer choices can automatically be eliminated. By concentrating on the author's main points (first and last lines), it is clear the passage is about the "new adventure" and "discovering himself". Answer choice (**B**) fits best.

Example 3-34

The author would most likely agree with which of the following statements?

(A) The natives of India feel imposed upon when strangers trod their land

(B) Most Americans view solidarity as a way to refresh their well-being

(C) The only way to survive a mid-life crisis is to escape reality

(D) Third-world countries are the perfect place to go camping

(E) Natural disasters are found in some of the poorest countries in the world

IMPROVING PARAGRAPH PROCESS

1. **R**ead only what's called for. The sentence is usually reproduced in the question.

    Read the first and last line of the passage for the main idea.

2. **E**liminate wrong answers first.

    Circle first words to help you find answers. There will be four wrong answers (slightly related) and one that makes perfect sense.

3. **V**ery concise

    The correct answer will very often be the shortest RESTATEMENT.

4. **I**ncorrect Punctuation

    The correct answer may call for correct punctuation. Remember all the previous rules regarding punctuation.

5. **S**ubjectivity is wrong

    There is only one right answer and it's found in the text.

6. **E**xtra, Contradicting, Obscure and Irrelevant Information

    All these previous problems could be in the wrong answer choices.

Here is an acronym to best help you remember how to approach the Improving Paragraph questions.

> **R** ead only essential parts
> **E** liminate wrong answers first
> **V** ery concise is the right answer
> **I** ncorrect punctuation is wrong
> **S** ubjectivity is wrong
> **E** xtra, confusing, irrelevant or contradictory info is wrong

Write **REVISE** at the top of your test page.

PART V:

SCHOLARSHIP SEARCH

THE SCHOLARSHIP SEARCH

NOW THAT YOU'VE TAKEN the SAT, practiced hard and received your ideal score, it's time to start looking for scholarships. College scholarship money is usually <u>awarded</u> to a student based on merit or winning a contest. Many colleges and universities offer scholarship opportunities based simply on a student's SAT score combined with his or her high school GPA. Below is a chart that represents how your SAT score can affect institutional financial aid. This chart represents the Math and Critical Reading section only.

SAT (Math/C Reading Scores)	REPRESENTS	POSSIBLE OUTCOME
800–950	high school equivalency	Junior College Entrance
960–1000	college ready	Moderate College Entrance
1100–1250	excellent preparation	Possible one-third to two-thirds scholarship to certain colleges
1260–1450	remarkable preparation	Possible "full ride" at mid-range colleges
1460–1600	extraordinary student	Possible "full ride" at high-end colleges

Many colleges give "full ride" scholarships to students with SAT scores starting around 1400 (Critical Reading and Math combined). If you receive scholarship money directly from the school, here are some tips to help get **more** scholarship money after they've decided your financial award.

1. Appeal for more money to the financial aid department. (Do this after you have received an award letter.)
2. Ask for any extra scholarship money that was awarded to students who decided not to attend the school. Ask to be considered in the re-awards that are usually distributed after the semester starts.
3. Many schools will give you more money if you raise your SAT score higher after you are already enrolled in school.

You should keep on friendly terms with the financial aid advisor during this process. Be sure to send him or her a thank-you note for working on your behalf.

FINDING OUTSIDE SCHOLARSHIPS

There are many scholarship opportunities outside of institutional aid.

There are many scholarship opportunities outside of institutional aid. It should be the goal of every student to apply for as many of these as possible. One can start searching for these scholarships by checking out with the web sites provided in this book. As you go, check off the sites you have visited, essays you've completed and responses you have gotten. You can also check with local high schools, organizations and community groups (e.g., religious institutions, private foundations, athletic clubs, Lions Club, parent's employer, veterans, etc.) for other scholarship contests. Only apply for those scholarships that you are qualified for.

The application/essay will be a representation of you and should convey who you are, where you are going and what you have to offer them (the college or those giving the scholarship). Many contest judges base their determinations solely on your essay/applications, since they will probably never meet you.

Example

Just call me Superwoman Extraordinaire. Not only have I been president of the Spanish Club, Captain of the Drill Team and Secretary of Student Government, but I've also maintained a 4.0 GPA, won volunteer of the year in my city and won four local art contests, all while working part-time as a cashier in a grocery store.

Your application/essay should immediately make an impression on the judges. This can be accomplished by offering a good "hook" at the beginning that will make them want to read on (remember, they will be reading/skimming numerous essays). Your "hook" should sum up who you are in just the first few sentences.

This will be your time to shine and to **SELL** yourself to the judges. Be specific about your accomplishments and talk about yourself every chance you get.

Stay away from negative topics. Your personal strengths should be conveyed but not compared to someone else's weaknesses. Avoid writing about misfortunes and hard times; judges tend to enjoy positive papers more.

Communicate how you can benefit the college/society by being a successful future leader if given the opportunity.

Do not be too quick to let the judges know about other scholarships you may have won. The judges usually want to give the scholarship money to applicants who **have not** already won a big contest.

Make sure you include ALL the volunteer work, leadership opportunities, awards won, extracurricular activities, works you have initiated, etc. in your application. The more of everything you enclose, the better. This includes several letters of recommendation from teachers, employers, church leaders, etc. (Make sure the letters are written on the letterhead of that company.)

Always sign the bottom of the essay and include a recent photograph of yourself. You will want to put a face to your name so the judges will remember you in their consideration.

If you are uncertain about what the scholarship judges are looking for, look at past scholarship winning essays or look on the Internet for creative or nontraditional winning essays. This can help give you ideas where to start with your essay.

Don't leave any blanks empty. If a question does not apply to you, write a N/A (for "not applicable") in the blank. Only use black ink when filling out your application/essay.

> **Stay away from negative topics. Your personal strengths should be conveyed but not compared to someone else's weaknesses.**

FUN TIP

You may consider typing your essay to really make it stand out. An actual typewriter can be found at most libraries.

LOANS AND GRANTS

If you're having a hard time finding good scholarships, don't worry. Scholarships usually make up less than 10 % of financial aid for most students. Generally about 40% comes from financial grants, and loans usually make up the remainder.

College loans are usually obtained by parents, with low interest, from the college, a bank or The College Board.

College loans are usually obtained by parents, with low interest, from the college, a bank or The College Board and must be paid back over time. Grant money is given to students based on need* and is on a first-come basis. Here is a list of grants that most students will be able to qualify for:

1. Federal Pell Grant: This is based on federal (FAFSA) guidelines and **MUST** be applied for early. (*If your first student has received a full scholarship, very often his or her Pell Grant can be applied and awarded to a second student—along with their own Pell Grant.*)
2. Federal Supplemental Education Opportunity Grant: Usually for the most needy, this can be applied for at the financial aid office.
3. State grants: Many states have free money, based on need, and they may also target studies in certain fields.
4. Institutional grants: These are from the schools and are sometimes given instead of a loan to encourage a student to come.

The earliest date to apply to FAFSA is January 1. This is first come—so apply early! For more information call (800) 433-3243 or go to the website www. fafsa.ed.gov.

*It is also a good idea to keep limited funds in your banking/savings account since this can be counted against monies given/awarded to you. Also, keep your resources detached from your parent's assets.

SCHOLARSHIP WEBSITES

THERE ARE MULTIPLE SCHOLARSHIPS and college resources available on the web. We have divided them into three major categories: organizations that offer scholarships, college resources and scholarship search sites. This list is by no means a comprehensive representation of all the scholarship resources available online, but hopefully it will give you a good starting point in your search for information.

There are multiple scholarships and college resources available on the web.

ORGANIZATIONS WITH SCHOLARSHIPS

There are several companies, organizations and funds that offer scholarships to college students. Check the links below to see if they offer any scholarships that may apply to you. Please note: some of the websites may require you to search for "Scholarship" in the index.

USDA: Animal and Plant Health Inspection Service
Scholarships for study in veterinary medicine and biomedical science
www.aphis.usda.gov

American Political Science Association
Scholarships and grants for research and study
www.apsanet.org

Ayn Rand Institute
Essay contest
www.aynrand.org/contest

Common Knowledge Scholarship Foundation
Scholarship contest based on quiz scores
www.cksf.org

Elks National Foundation
Scholarships for leadership and Elks legacy
www.elks.org/enf

Kohl's Corporation
Scholarships for volunteer service
www.kohlscorporation.com

Microsoft Careers
Scholarships for computer science and related technical disciplines
https://careers.microsoft.com/careers/en/us/collegescholarship.aspx

Hispanic Scholarship Fund
Scholarships for many types of degrees
www.hsf.net

National Collegiate Athletic Association
Scholarship and internships for athletes
www.ncaa.org

The Roothbert Fund, Inc.
Scholarships for students with spiritual values
www.roothbertfund.org

Siemens Foundation
Scholarship competition for math, science and technology
www.siemens-foundation.org

Thurgood Marshall College Fund
Scholarships for the 47 TMCF Colleges and Universities
www.thurgoodmarshallfund.net

COLLEGE RESOURCES

Upromise
Earn scholarship money by making everyday restaurant or grocery purchases
www.upromise.com

Wall Street Journal: Education
Latest news about university education and financial resources
www.collegejournal.com

College Savings Plan Network
Information about developing a 529 Plan
www.collegesavings.org

GrantsNet
Database of searchable grants
www.grantsnet.org

Foundation Grants to Individuals Online
Resource for finding grants
www.gtionline.fdncenter.org

National Association of Student Financial Aid Administrators
Information regarding laws and regulations of financial aid
www.nasfaa.org

Sallie Mae
Information about student loans
www.salliemae.com

City of College Dreams
Resource for all types of college information
www.cityofcollegedreams.org

College for Texans
Resource guide for universities in Texas
www.collegefortexans.com

Federal Student Aid
Information about programs and resources from the U.S. Department of Education
www.federalstudentaid.ed.gov

Guaranteed Scholarships
An alphabetical listing of scholarship offers from colleges across the nation
www.guaranteed-scholarships.com

SCHOLARSHIP & UNIVERSITY DATABASES

There is a multitude of websites available that allow students to research scholarships and universities. Below is a list of some of the most popular ones. Each is put into a grid to help you utilize these resources to the best of your ability. As you find scholarships, feel free to note the name of the scholarship, the deadline, whether an essay is required and the date you mail the application. This will help you keep track of your work.

Scholarship Web Sites	Contest Name	Deadline	Application	Essay	Mailed
www.adventuresineducation.org/ sbase	1._____	_____	_____	_____	_____
	2._____	_____	_____	_____	_____
	3._____	_____	_____	_____	_____
	4._____	_____	_____	_____	_____
	5._____	_____	_____	_____	_____

Scholarship Web Sites	Contest Name	Deadline	Application	Essay	Mailed
www.BrokeScholar.com	1._____	_____	_____	_____	_____
	2._____	_____	_____	_____	_____
	3._____	_____	_____	_____	_____
	4._____	_____	_____	_____	_____
	5._____	_____	_____	_____	_____
www.careertools.org/scholarship	1._____	_____	_____	_____	_____
	2._____	_____	_____	_____	_____
	3._____	_____	_____	_____	_____
	4._____	_____	_____	_____	_____
	5._____	_____	_____	_____	_____
www.collegeispossible.org	1._____	_____	_____	_____	_____
	2._____	_____	_____	_____	_____
	3._____	_____	_____	_____	_____
	4._____	_____	_____	_____	_____
	5._____	_____	_____	_____	_____

Scholarship Web Sites	Contest Name	Deadline	Application	Essay	Mailed
www.collegenet.com	1._____ 2._____ 3._____ 4._____ 5._____	_____ _____ _____ _____ _____	_____ _____ _____ _____ _____	_____ _____ _____ _____ _____	_____ _____ _____ _____ _____
www.collegexpress.com	1._____ 2._____ 3._____ 4._____ 5._____	_____ _____ _____ _____ _____	_____ _____ _____ _____ _____	_____ _____ _____ _____ _____	_____ _____ _____ _____ _____
www.fastaid.com	1._____ 2._____ 3._____ 4._____ 5._____	_____ _____ _____ _____ _____	_____ _____ _____ _____ _____	_____ _____ _____ _____ _____	_____ _____ _____ _____ _____

Scholarship Web Sites	Contest Name	Deadline	Application	Essay	Mailed
www.Fastweb.com	1._____	_____	_____	_____	_____
	2._____	_____	_____	_____	_____
	3._____	_____	_____	_____	_____
	4._____	_____	_____	_____	_____
	5._____	_____	_____	_____	_____
www.freschinfo.com	1._____	_____	_____	_____	_____
	2._____	_____	_____	_____	_____
	3._____	_____	_____	_____	_____
	4._____	_____	_____	_____	_____
	5._____	_____	_____	_____	_____
www.gocollege.com	1._____	_____	_____	_____	_____
	2._____	_____	_____	_____	_____
	3._____	_____	_____	_____	_____
	4._____	_____	_____	_____	_____
	5._____	_____	_____	_____	_____

Scholarship Web Sites	Contest Name	Deadline	Application	Essay	Mailed
http://apps.collegeboard.com/cbsearch_ss/welcome.jsp	1._____ 2._____ 3._____ 4._____ 5._____	_____ _____ _____ _____ _____	_____ _____ _____ _____ _____	_____ _____ _____ _____ _____	_____ _____ _____ _____ _____
http://aid.military.com/scholarship/search-for-scholarships.do	1._____ 2._____ 3._____ 4._____ 5._____	_____ _____ _____ _____ _____	_____ _____ _____ _____ _____	_____ _____ _____ _____ _____	_____ _____ _____ _____ _____
www.petersons.com	1._____ 2._____ 3._____ 4._____ 5._____	_____ _____ _____ _____ _____	_____ _____ _____ _____ _____	_____ _____ _____ _____ _____	_____ _____ _____ _____ _____

Scholarship Web Sites	Contest Name	Deadline	Application	Essay	Mailed
www.scholarship-page.com	1._____	_____	_____	_____	_____
	2._____	_____	_____	_____	_____
	3._____	_____	_____	_____	_____
	4._____	_____	_____	_____	_____
	5._____	_____	_____	_____	_____
www.Scholarships.com	1._____	_____	_____	_____	_____
	2._____	_____	_____	_____	_____
	3._____	_____	_____	_____	_____
	4._____	_____	_____	_____	_____
	5._____	_____	_____	_____	_____
www.scholarshipscanada.com	1._____	_____	_____	_____	_____
	2._____	_____	_____	_____	_____
	3._____	_____	_____	_____	_____
	4._____	_____	_____	_____	_____
	5._____	_____	_____	_____	_____

Scholarship Web Sites	Contest Name	Deadline	Application	Essay	Mailed
StudentAwards.com	1._____ 2._____ 3._____ 4._____ 5._____	_____ _____ _____ _____ _____	_____ _____ _____ _____ _____	_____ _____ _____ _____ _____	_____ _____ _____ _____ _____
www.supercollege.com	1._____ 2._____ 3._____ 4._____ 5._____	_____ _____ _____ _____ _____	_____ _____ _____ _____ _____	_____ _____ _____ _____ _____	_____ _____ _____ _____ _____
www.collegeanswer.com	1._____ 2._____ 3._____ 4._____ 5._____	_____ _____ _____ _____ _____	_____ _____ _____ _____ _____	_____ _____ _____ _____ _____	_____ _____ _____ _____ _____

Scholarship Web Sites	Contest Name	Deadline	Application	Essay	Mailed
www.Financialaidofficer.com	1._____	_____	_____	_____	_____
	2._____	_____	_____	_____	_____
	3._____	_____	_____	_____	_____
	4._____	_____	_____	_____	_____
	5._____	_____	_____	_____	_____
www.finaid.org	1._____	_____	_____	_____	_____
	2._____	_____	_____	_____	_____
	3._____	_____	_____	_____	_____
	4._____	_____	_____	_____	_____
	5._____	_____	_____	_____	_____
www.studentaid.com	1._____	_____	_____	_____	_____
	2._____	_____	_____	_____	_____
	3._____	_____	_____	_____	_____
	4._____	_____	_____	_____	_____
	5._____	_____	_____	_____	_____

SCHOLARSHIPS FOR STUDY ABROAD AND INTERNATIONAL PROGRAMS

Scholarship Web Sites	Contest Name	Deadline	Application	Essay	Mailed
www.iefa.org	1._____				
	2._____				
	3._____				
	4._____				
	5._____				
www.iesabroad.org	1._____				
	2._____				
	3._____				
	4._____				
	5._____				
www.internationalscholarships.com	1._____				
	2._____				
	3._____				
	4._____				
	5._____				

Scholarship Web Sites	Contest Name	Deadline	Application	Essay	Mailed
www.internationalstudent.com/	1._____	_____	_____	_____	_____
	2._____	_____	_____	_____	_____
	3._____	_____	_____	_____	_____
	4._____	_____	_____	_____	_____
	5._____	_____	_____	_____	_____

This compilation is in no way an endorsement of any particular website. The inclusion or omission of any particular website does not reflect the beliefs or opinions of *College Prep Genius* or Maven of Memory Publishing. These websites are reproduced for your benefit. This listing is for informational purposes only and is no way a guarantee of scholarship awards.

PART VI:

JOURNAL FOR
TEST SUCCESS

WHY KEEP A JOURNAL?

SINCE THE SAT AND PSAT/NMQT are standardized tests that have recurring patterns, the key to doing well is to practice recognizing the hidden patterns and using strategies to find the correct answers. The Journal for Test Success is a way for you to keep records of how you're progressing. As you take practice exams, you should fill out the journal pages with the questions that you missed.

When you miss a question, it should be your goal to conquer that pattern; the next time you take that particular practice test or when that pattern arises again, you can then know how to conquer it.

These are tests of logic, reasoning and critical thinking. You need to train your mind to look for the correct answer by exposing the patterns and observing the relationships between the question and its answer.

> **The Journal for Test Success is a way for you to keep records of how you're progressing.**

Here is how to use these journal pages

1. Make copies of the journal pages and put them in a notebook.
2. Keep a record of testing dates and scores on the Test Record page.
3. When you miss a question, rewrite it and its answers on the corresponding page.
4. Rework it correctly; find out why you missed it or worked it the long way.
5. Review the missed questions periodically to ensure you can still answer them correctly and quickly.
   > Once a month (for minimal recall)
   > Once a week (for a good refresher)
   > Nightly (for optimal review)
6. Compare your improvements the next time you take the same test.

7. Practice writing at least one essay a week.

    Reuse and recycle the same examples to fit the topic.

    Make sure it contains all the elements in the acronym.

8. Form a study group with others who will be practicing for the tests.

    Conduct friendly competitions (weekly, bi-weekly).

    Divide into groups (boys vs. girls, etc.) .

    Reward the individual and the group with the best improvement.

TEST RECORD

Date	Prep Book	Test #	Critical Reading Score	Math Score	Writing Score	Total Score

CRITICAL READING

(Sentence Completion)   COMPLETION

Test #	Problem	Answer Choices	Answer Details
Date		(A)	
		(B)	
Page #		(C)	
		(D)	
Quest. #		(E)	
Date		(A)	
		(B)	
Page #		(C)	
		(D)	
Quest. #		(E)	
Date		(A)	
		(B)	
Page #		(C)	
		(D)	
Quest. #		(E)	
Date		(A)	
		(B)	
Page #		(C)	
		(D)	
Quest. #		(E)	

CRITICAL READING

(Passage-Based Reading)

CITATION, USE, PASSAGE, DUAL

Test #	Problem	Answer Choices	Answer Details
Date		(A)	
		(B)	
Page #		(C)	
		(D)	
Quest. #		(E)	
Date		(A)	
		(B)	
Page #		(C)	
		(D)	
Quest. #		(E)	
Date		(A)	
		(B)	
Page #		(C)	
		(D)	
Quest. #		(E)	
Date		(A)	
		(B)	
Page #		(C)	
		(D)	
Quest. #		(E)	

MATH

(Multiple-Choice)   EASY MATH

Test #	Problem	Answer Choices	Answer Details
Date		(A)	
		(B)	
Page #		(C)	
		(D)	
Quest. #		(E)	
Date		(A)	
		(B)	
Page #		(C)	
		(D)	
Quest. #		(E)	
Date		(A)	
		(B)	
Page #		(C)	
		(D)	
Quest. #		(E)	
Date		(A)	
		(B)	
Page #		(C)	
		(D)	
Quest. #		(E)	

MATH

(Student Response)

EASY MATH

Test #	Problem	Grid-in Box	Answer Details
Date			
Page #			
Quest. #			
Date			
Page #			
Quest. #			
Date			
Page #			
Quest. #			
Date			
Page #			
Quest. #			

WRITING

(Sentence Error)

ABCDE S P O T & A I D WORD PROBLEM

Test #	Problem	Answer Details
Date Page # Quest. #		
Date Page # Quest. #		
Date Page # Quest. #		
Date Page # Quest. #		

WRITING

(Improving Paragraphs)   REVISE

Test #	Problem	Answer Choices	Answer Details
Date		(A)	
		(B)	
Page #		(C)	
		(D)	
Quest. #		(E)	
Date		(A)	
		(B)	
Page #		(C)	
		(D)	
Quest. #		(E)	
Date		(A)	
		(B)	
Page #		(C)	
		(D)	
Quest. #		(E)	
Date		(A)	
		(B)	
Page #		(C)	
		(D)	
Quest. #		(E)	

WRITING

(Improving Sentences)   RESTATEMENT

Test #	Problem	Answer Choices	Answer Details
Date		(A)	
		(B)	
Page #		(C)	
		(D)	
Quest. #		(E)	
Date		(A)	
		(B)	
Page #		(C)	
		(D)	
Quest. #		(E)	
Date		(A)	
		(B)	
Page #		(C)	
		(D)	
Quest. #		(E)	
Date		(A)	
		(B)	
Page #		(C)	
		(D)	
Quest. #		(E)	

PRACTICE ESSAY - Topic

H

O

T

P

O

W

E

R

F

U

L

P

A

P

E

R

APPENDIX A

Prefixes, Root Words and Suffixes

Pos Prefix	Definitions	Examples
am	friend	amicable—friendly
amphi	two	amphora—a jar with two handles
ben	good	benefit—promoting well-being
bene	well	beneficent—producing good
con	together	congregation—a gathering of persons
cred	belief	credulous—ready to believe
dyn	power	dyne—a unit of force
dynamo	power	dynamic—having explosive force
em	into	empower—give power to
en	make into	enchant—make magical
eu	pleasant	eulogy—words or praise
hyper	over	hyperacusia—abnormally acute hearing
intra	within	intragroup—within a group
macro	large	macrotous—having large ears
magni	large	magnificent—great in deed
neo	new	neophyte—beginner
omni	all	omniscient—all knowing
para	beside	parallel—laying side by side
pro	forward	procedure—method of going towards a goal
super	above	supercilious—proud
supr	great	supreme—of the highest quality
sur	over	surcoat—overcoat
syl	together	syllable—one or more letters which form one sound
sym	along with	symbolize—to present a symbol
syn	along with	synthesis—a combination of parts to make a whole
sys	with	system—a method
ultra	beyond	ultrasonic—beyond sound
vita	long life	vitality—vigor in living
viv	life	vivacious—lively character

Neg Prefix	Definitions	Examples
a	in	abed—in the bed
a	without	amorphous—without shape
ab	not	abnormal—not being normal
an	absence of	anemia—not enough red blood cells
ante	against	antebellum—before the war
anti	opposite	anti-Semitic—against the Jews
apo	away from	apocope—a cutting off
beli	warlike	bellicose—inclined to start wars

Neg Prefix	Definitions	Examples
cata	down	catagenesis—evolution going backwards
contra	opposite	contraception—against conceiving
contro	against	controversy—opposite views
counter	opposite	counterclockwise—going in a direction opposite of clockwise
de	down from	denounce—putting down
di	two	dichotomy—a separation into two parts
dis	not	dislike—to not like
dys	poor	dysfunctional—functioning poorly
e	out	eject—to throw out
ec	out	eclipse—to hide
ef	out	effete—worn out
ex	out of	expect—to look out for
hypo	too little	hypoallergenic—having little likelihood of causing an allergic reaction
hyper	too much	hypersensitive/overly sensitive
Il	not	illegal—not legal
Im	not	immature—not mature
In	not	innocent—not guilty
Ir	not	irresponsible—not responsible
mal	evil	malicious—having evil intentions
male	bad	maladjusted—ill adjusted
mis	wrong	mispronounce—pronounce incorrectly
miso	hate	misogyny—hating women
mor	die	mortuary—place for dead
non	not	nonabrasive—not abrasive
ob	against	obviate—prevent a situation
of	against	offense—go against the law
pseudo	false	pseudodox—a false opinion
se	apart	secret—something hidden
un	not	uninformed—not informed

Neutral Prefix	Definition	Examples
ad	to	addict—towards a habit
amb	about	ambidexter—one who uses both hands with skill
ambi	around	amble—to walk leisurely about
ana	up	anabasis—a journey upward
be	intensive	bedeck—to cover up
bi	two	biceps—large muscle fastened in two places
bin	two	binocular—an instrument with two eyes
bis	twice	bisection—something divided into two equal parts

Neutral Prefix	Definition	Examples
circ	around	circumspect—to look around
circum	around	circumfluous—flowing around
demi	half	demisuit—half armor
dia	through	dialysis—the separation into elements
em	in	embalm—to insert preservatives
en	into	encamp—set up camp
epi	upon	epidemic—a spreading among people
hemi	half	hemisphere—half of a globe
inter	among	interaction—action for mutual advantage
intro	into	introduce—lead into
mon	one	monad—a unit
mono	one	monodrama—a play with one actor
per	through	perceive—to understand
peri	around	pericardium—around the heart
post	after	postfix—to add to end of syllable or word
pre	before	preamble—an introduction
re	back	rebuild—build again
semi	half	semicircle—a half circle
sesqui	one and a half	sesquicentennial—relating to a century and a half
sub	under	subaltern—under another
trans	across	transatlantic—across the Atlantic

Root Word	Definition	Examples
acer	bitter	acerate—shaped like a needle
acid	sour	acidic—acid building
acri	sharp	acrid—stingingly bitter
ag	do	demagogue—one who stirs people up for profit
agi	move	agenda—the program of work to be done
ago	go	agitate—keep moving
ali	other	alias—an assumed name
allo	other	allograph—forgery
alter	other	alternative—another choice
anni	year	annual—relating to a year
annu	year	anniversary—the annual return of an event or a day
anthrop	man	misanthropy—hatred of mankind
arch	ruler	genarch—the head of the family
aster	star	asterisk—a tiny star
astro	star	astrophile—one interested in star lore
aud	hear	audible—can be heard

Root Word	Definition	Examples
aus	listen	auscultation—the act of listening to sounds within the body
aut	self	automat—a self-service cafeteria
auto	self	autocrat—an absolute monarch
bene	well	benefit—an advantage
bio	life	biology—the study of living organisms
bon	good	bonny—sweet and attractive
calor	heat	caloric—like heat
cap	take	capias—a writ for arrest
capit	head	capital—amount of accumulated goods
capt	chief	captain—the head
cause	cause	accuser—one who charges another with a crime
cede	go	cede—to yield
ceed	yield	abscess—a localized collection of pus due to infection
cep	receive	exception—something left out of general use
cept	take	interception—to gain possession
cess	surrender	recession—act of going back
chrom	color	chromophilic—easy to stain
chron	time	chronic—continuing for a long time
cide	kill	fratricide—the killing of one's brother
cise	cut	incise—cut into
civ	citizen	civil—trained
claim	declare	clamor—a shouting
clam	call out	exclaim—cry out
clud	shut	recluse—one who shuts himself
clus	shut	include—to take in
congnosc	know	cognition—the act of knowing
coni	dust	otoconia—ear dust
cor	heart	core—the heart
cord	heart	cordial—cheerful
corp	body	corpse—a dead body
corpor	body	corporal—relating to the body
cour	heart	courage—to have heart; bravery
crea	create	creant—having the urge to create
cred	believe	credo—set of opinions
cub	lean back	accubation—posture of lying down
cumb	lie down	encumber—to place a burden upon
cus	motive	excuse—the reason for an action
cuse	motive	causal—relating to motive

Root Word	Definition	Examples
cycl	wheel	cyclical—moving in a circle of cycle
cyclo	circle	cyclitis—inflammation of the tissue behind the eyeball
dem	people	demophile—a friend of the people
demo	people	democrat—one who believe in democracy
dent	tooth	dental—relating to teeth
dic	say	dictacte—command
dict	declare	diction—language
dont	tooth	orthodontia—straightening of irregular teeth
dorm	sleep	dormancy—state of being static
drome	running	prodrome—an early warning of disease
dromos	running	hippodromist—a circus rider
duc	lead	abduct—to take away
duce	lead	induce—to persuade
duct	lead	educate—to develop
end	within	endoral—within the mouth
endo	within	endotrophic—nourished from within
enni	year	sexennial—occuring once every six years
fac	make	factive—making
fact	make	facsimile—a copy that is exact in every detail
feal	faith	fealties—intense fidelity
fect	make	proficient—able to do things well
feder	trust	federal—united
fer	bring	deference—respect for
fic	make	affect—make an impression upon
fid	faith	infidel—one who has no faith
fide	faith	fealty—loyalty
fila	thread	filate—slender
fili	thread	filet—lace made of fine threads
fin	end	final—relating to the end
finis	end	confine—to keep shut in
fix	fix	fixate—to become fixed
flect	bend	flection—the act of bending
flex	bend	flexible—able to bend
flu	flowing	fluid—a liquid
fluc	flowing	flue—a passageway for a flow of air
fluv	flowing	fluvial—in relation to a moving stream
flux	flowing	fluxion—the act of changing
forc	strong	fort—a stronghold for protection

Root Word	Definition	Examples
fort	fortune	fortress—a fortified place
fortuna	chance	fortuitous—happening by chance
fum	smoke	fumy—smoke-like; a funny smell
ge	earth	geobios—life of earth
gen	race	general—relating to all kinds
geo	soil	geophilous—growing or living on or under ground
germ	vital part	germin—to bud
gest	carry	gestant—pregnant
gnosi	know	agnosy—state of not knowing
grad	step	grado—a degree of a scale in music
graph	write	graphite—soft, black carbon used for pencils
grat	pleasing	gratify—to please
grav	heavy	grave—serious
gravi	weighty	gravid—pregnant
gravito	heavy	graviton—a hypothetical particle with zero charge
gred	degree	gradual—processing by small steps
greg	herd	aggregate—to collect
gress	walk	ingress—the act of entering
hab	have	habitat—the natural abode of a plant or animal
habit	live	habile—able
helio	sun	heliod—like the sun
hema	blood	hemoid—like blood
hemo	blood	hemoptoe—hemorrhage of the lungs
hum	earth	humus—earth
human	ground	humble—lowly
hydr	water	hydrotherapy—the therapeutic use of water
hydra	water	hydrophobia—morbid fear of water
hydro	water	hydraulic—acting by water power
hypn	sleep	hypnobate—a sleepwalker
hypno	sleep	hypnotic—soporific
intellect	power to know	intellectualisms—devotion to the exercise of intellect
intellig	power to know and think	intelligent—having the power to think and know
jac	throw	dejected—low in spirits
jec	lie	eject—to throw out
ject	throw	projection—the act of thrusting forward
join	join	conjoin—unite
jud	judge	judicial—relating to administration judicial power
judi	lawyer	abjudicate—reject the case

Root Word	Definition	Examples
judic	judge	injudicious—not having sound judgment
junct	join	junction—act of joining; place of meeting
jur	law	conjure—to swear together
jus	law	adjustive—tending to put into proper order
koni	dust	koniscope—an instrument for estimating the dust in the atmosphere
laut	wash	ablaut—a systematic variation of vowels in the same root or affix
lav	wash	lavish—flowing like water
leg	law	legal—lawful
letter	letters	letterpress—the process of printing from an inked raised surface
liber	free	liberal—relating to freedom
lic	permit	license—freedom to act
licit	permit	illicit—illegal
lit	letters	literal—according with the letter of the scriptures
liter	letters	literacy—the state of being educated
litera	letters	litany—a prayer consisting of invocations and responses
liver	free	delivery—freedom; liberation
loc	speak	soliloquy—a long speech to oneself
loco	place	dislocate—to move away from its place
log	word	logograph—a word puzzle
logo	word	logical—reasonable
loqui	speak	elocute—speak out in public
lot	wash	immunoblot—radioactively labeled antibody is used as the molecular probe
luc	light	lucid—clear
lum	light	luminary—a heavenly body
lun	light	lunacies—intermittent insanity believed to be related to the moon
lus	light	luster—a glow of light from within
lut	wash	launder—to wash and iron clothes
magna	great	magnify—to intensify
magni	great	magnum—great; in size, a large bottle of wine
man	by hand	manifest—seen at hand
manu	by hand	manual—relating to the hand
mar.	sea	marine—a sailor
mari	pool	mere—a lake
matri	mother	matrix—the womb
matric	mother	matricide—the murder of one's mother
matro	mother	matronymic—mother of one's ancestor
medi	half	mediate—come between
mega	large	megadont—having large teeth

Root Word	Definition	Examples
megalo	large	megascopic—enlarged
mem	remember	memory—the ability to recall
mer	sea	merman—mythical male sea creature
meter	measure	mete—to measure
micro	small	microbe—a minute organism or germ
migra	wander	migrate—to wander
mis	wrong	misadventure—an accident
miso	bad	misalliance—an improper union
miss	bad	missile—something which can be sent through the air
mitt	send	remit—pay back
mob	move	mobile—capable of moving
monstr	show	monstrous-extreme
monstri	show	demonstrate—to display
mors	death	remorse—torture of conscience
mort/mori	death	mortuous—deathlike
mot	move	motive—cause
mov	move	removable—able to be taken or carried away
multi	much	multifold—folded many times
multus	many	multiple—consisting of more than one
must	show	muster—to put on display
nasc	to be born	renascent—to be reborn
nat	to spring forth	natal—relating to birth
neo	new	neolatry—the worship of the new
neur	nerve	neurism—nerve force
nounc	warn	denounce—accuse
November	new	novalia—new-plowed fields
number	number	numerant—used in counting
numer	number	numerous—of great number
nunci	declare	enunciate—to pronounce carefully
omni	all	omnify—enlarge
oper	work	opera—a drama set to music
opus	work	opuscule—a small petty work
oss	bone	ossify—to make into bone
osteo	bone	osteal—relating to bone; osteoporosis
pac	please	pacer—calm
pan	all	panacea—a cure for all ills
pater	father	patron—a wealthy person who supports a cause or a person; patriot
patr	father	paternal—relating to a father; paternity

Root Word	Definition	Examples
ped	foot	pedantry—display of learning
pel	drive	pulse—heartbeat; pulmonary
pen	hang	impending—hanging over one, as in doom
pend	hang	pendant—hanging
phil	love	philliter—a love potion
phila	love	philanthropist—a lover of mankind
phile	love	philematology—the science of kissing
philo	love	philomuse—a lover of poetry and arts
photo	light	photon—a unit of light intensity
pict	paint	depict—to form a likeness
picto	paint	pictury—tending to look like a picture; pictograph
plais	please	implacable—cannot be soothed
plu	more	plural—more than one
plur	more	plurennial—a plant living many years
plus	think	nonplussed—perplexed
pneuma	breath	pneumonia—a disease of the lungs
pneumon	breath	pneumatic—pertaining to air
pod	foot	podium—a platform
poly	many	polyanthus—a type of plant
pon	set	to set forth to float; pontoon
pop	people	populace—the people
port	carry	portable—able to be carried
portion	part	portion—the one who divides
pos	place	posit—set firmly in place
posse	power	possessorship—complete ownership
poten	power	potent—powerful; potential
potes	power	possible—able to be
pound	power	impoundment—refusal of the presidents of the United States to spend money
prim	first	primal—original
prime	first	primacy—state of being first in rank
puls	push	expulsion—drive out
punct	point	punctuate—to place a point at the end of a sentence
put	think	compute—to calculate
ri	laughter	riantly—laughingly; hilarious
ridi	laughter	ridicule—laughter at the expense of another
risi	laughter	risible—to dispose to laughter
rog	beg	derogate—to lessen
roga	ask	arrogant—proud

Root Word	Definition	Examples
sangui	blood	sanguine—confident
sat	enough	satisfy—to give pleasure
satis	enough	saturate—to soak thoroughly
scope	watch	telescope—instrument for viewing distant objects
scrib	write	scribble—meaningless writings
scrip	write	conscript—to be drafted into military service
sign	sign	signate—sign or seal expressing authority
signi	mark	design—intention; signify
silic	flint	silica—silicon dioxide
simil	like	similize—to compare; similar
simul	resembling	simulate—pretend
sist	stand	persist-stand firmly
soph	wisdom	sophic—full of wisdom
spec	watch	specious—pleasing to the eye but deceptive
spect	see	spectacle—a show
spectro	observe	spectrohelioscope—instrument to view the sun
sphere	ball	atmosphere—the mass of air surrounding the earth
spond	answer	respond—to answer in kind
spons	pledge	sponsor—to assume responsibility
sta	stand	standard—established
stereo	solid	stereotype—anything reproduced without variation
stet	stand	stethogoniometer—apparatus for measuring curvature of the chest; stethoscope
stit	stand	persist—stand firmly
stru	build	construe—to explain
struct	build	construct—to build
sume	take	assume—to suppose
sump	use	consume—to use up
tact	touch	tactus—the sense of touch; tactile
tain	hold together	containment—prevention of hostile incurment
tang	touch	intangibility—quality of not being touched
techni	skill	technicality—a detail of skill and procedure
technic	art	pyrotechnics—a fireworks show
tempo	time	contemporary—those who lived at the same time
tempor	time	temporal—limited by time; temporary
ten	hold	tenant—occupant; tenacious
tend	stretch	extend—stretch forth
tens	strain	intensify—quality of strain
tent	hold together	maintain—to keep up

Root Word	Definition	Examples
tent	strain	detente—relaxation of strained relations
test	to bear witness	testate—leaving a valid will which has been witnessed; testament
the	God	thearchy—government under God
theo	God	theology—the study of elements of religions
tig	touch	contiguous—touching; in contact
ting	touch	contingency—possibility
tinu	hold	continually—without stopping
tract	draw	traction—the act of pulling
trah	pull	detract—to draw away from
trib	pay	contribute—to give money to a cause
tuit	teach	tutoriate—a body of tutors; tuition
tut	guard	tutor—one who teaches a pupil
ultima	last	ultimate—final
uni	one	unify—make into one
vac	empty	vacate—to make empty
vale	strength	valediction—a farewell
vali	worth	validate—establish legitimacy
valu	valor	valuation—estimation of worth
ven	come	adventure—a remarkable experience; ventral; ventriliquist
veni	come	event—a happening
vent	come	adventitious—not usual
ver	true	veracity—truth
veri	genuine	veridify—genuineness
vers	turn	versus—against as in legal actions
vert	turn	divert—turn attention away from
vest	clothe	vested—clothed in authority
vic	change	vicarial—relating to a vicar
vicis	substitute	vicarious—being substituted; vicissitude
vict	conquer	victor—winner
vid	see	video—visual part of television
vinc	conquer	vincible—being overtaken
vis	see	vision—something seen
vita	life	vitamin—of the essential constituents
viv	alive	vivacious—lively in temper
vivi	live	vivid—sharp/clear
volcan	fire	volcano—a mountain erupting molten lava
vulcan	fire	vulcanist—a metal worker

Suffixes	Definition	Examples
able	able	capable—able to do things well
ad	result of action	myriad—a collective number
ada	result of action	armada—a fleet of warships
ade	result of action	blockade—the act of isolating an enemy
age	act of	carriage—the act of carrying oneself
al	relating to	sensual—relating to the senses
an	native of	American—a native of America
ance	action	assistance—the act of giving help
ancy	process	militancy—a fighting spirit
ar	one who	burglar—one who commits burglary
ary	relating to	burglary—the act of breaking in
asis	condition	oasis—fertile condition
ata	result of action	enigmata—something hard to understand
ate	cause	dedicate—to set apart with a purpose
cian	having a certain skill	logician—an expert in the science of logic
cule	very small	reticule—a small net handbag
dom	quality	freedom—state of being free
ee	one who receives the action	employee—paid for action
en	made	silken—made of silk
ence	action	difference—state of being unlike
ency	state	efficiency—the ability to get things done
er	that which	reporter—one who reports
ery	quality	bakery—a place where food is baked
esis	process	genesis—act of coming into being
ful	full of	frightful—able to make one full of terror
fy	make	vitrify—to make into glass
ian	relating to	Orwellian—resembling the work of George Orwell
ible	can do	credible—can be believed
ic	nature of	endemic—native to a particular people or country
icle	very small	funicle—a small cord
ile	suited for	docile—easy to teach
ine	nature of	divine—godly
ion	act of	diction—choice of words
ish	origin	boorish—a lout
ism	doctrine	alcoholism—a condition of addiction to alcohol
ist	one who	alarmist—one who excites alarms needlessly
ite	quality of	appetite—craving
ity	state of	amenity—state of being pleasant

Suffixes	Definition	Examples
ive	causing	declarative—tending to make a statement
ize	make	acclimatize—to adapt to a new condition
less	without	careless—without care
ling	very small	duckling—a baby duck
ly	like	listlessly—like one who is without spirit
ment	act of	attainment—state of having reached a goal
ness	state of	baselessness—the state of being baseless
oid	like	asteroid—like a star
logy	study	biology—the study of living creatures
or	one who	exhibitor—one who shows things
ory	place where	factory—a place for manufacturing
osis	action	osmosis—the diffusion of fluid through a semi-permeable membrane
ous	full of	delicious—having a delightful taste
ship	office	hardship—suffering
sion	state of	confusion—state of being confused
tion	result of	reflection—an image thrown back
tude	condition of	similitude—the condition of likeness
ty	quality	plenty—quality of having much
ure	act	censure—to blame
y	inclined	faulty—inclined to be at fault

Appendix B:

Math Terms

MATH TERMS

THE TABLE BELOW INCLUDES some of the most important math terms and rules. Learning and memorizing the following terms and rules is essential to doing well on the Math portion of the SAT and PSAT/NMSQT. The best way to make sure you understand each rule is to make an example of the rule in the table. Feel free to draw diagrams or make equations to guarantee that you familiarize yourself with the rules. Make a check by each rule once you've learned it.

Math Terminology	Definition/Properties	Make an Example	Know It √
1 to 1 Ratio	A ratio that is equivalent to one.		
30–60–90 Triangle	A right triangle with interior angles equal to 30°–60°– 90°. The length of each side will follow the ratio 1:2: √3.		
360 Degrees	The sum of the central angles in a circle.		
45–45–90 Triangle	If two of three interior angles equal 45º, then the third angle equals 90°. The hypotenuse will be the length of one side multiplied by the square root of 2.		
90-Degree Angle	The right angle formed by perpendicular lines, segments and rays.		
Absolute Value	The distance of a number from the origin (e.g., –5 and 5 have an absolute value of 5).		
Abstract Fractional Equation	A fractional equation where all or most of the terms are different variables .		
Acute Angle	An angle that measures more than 0 degrees and less than 90 degrees		
Additive Identity	Zero (since 0 + a = a).		
Additive Inverse	For any number a, a + (-a) = 0		

Math Terminology	Definition/Properties	Make an Example	Know It √
Adjacent Angles	Two angles that share the same side or vertex.		
Algebraic Expression	An expression having at least one variable; they can be added, subtracted, multiplied and divided.		
Alternate Interior Angles	For two lines cut by a transversal, a pair of nonadjacent angles located between the two lines and on opposite sides of the transversal		
Altitude	A line segment that extends from one vertex or a plane to the opposite side, forming a right angle.		
Angle Bisector	A ray, line or segment that passes through the vertex of an angle and divides the angle into two equal parts.		
Angle	Two rays joined by their endpoints.		
Arc	A portion of a circle; the measure of the central angle (circle) $2x$ measure of the inscribed angle.		
Area	A two-dimensional space covered by a flat object.		
Area of a Circle $A = \pi r^2$	The product of 3.14 times the radius of the circle squared.		
Area of a Square	The product of one of the sides of the square squared $(A = S^2)$.		
Area of a Rectangle	The product of the length and the width $(A = L \times W)$.		
Arithmetic Sequence	A sequence in which the difference between any two consecutive terms are the same.		
Arithmetic Series	The sum of the terms of an arithmetic sequence.		
Arrangement	An ordered grouping of elements.		
Associate Property	For any real numbers a, b, and c: $(a + b) + c = a + (b + c)$ and $(a \times b) \times c = a \times (b \times c)$.		

Math Terminology	Definition/Properties	Make an Example	Know It √
Average	The sum of a set of values divided by the number of values. **Weighted Average**—instead of each of the data points contributing equally to the final average, some data points contribute more than others. **Combined Average**—taking the average totals of a group of two or more and adding them together and dividing by the total of members.		
Axiom	A statement assumed to be true without proof.		
Balance	A remaining amount.		
Base	The bottom-part measurement of a triangle used to calculate the area.		
Base Angle	An acute angle that's opposite the congruent sides.		
Bar Chart	A chart with rectangular bars with lengths proportional to the values that they represent. They're used for comparing two or more values that were taken over time or on different conditions, usually on small data sets.		
Binomial	A quantity consisting of the sum or difference of two monomials.		
Bisect	To divide into two congruent parts.		
c times	*as old as* Jim = ($c \times$ Jim's age)		
Capacity	The maximum amount that a 3-dimensional object can hold.		
Center	The point in the interior of a circle from which all points are equidistant.		
Central Angle	An angle with vertex at the center of a circle.		
Chord	A segment having endpoints on a circle.		

Math Terminology	Definition/Properties	Make an Example	Know It √
Circle	A set of points on a plane that are halfway from a single point (also called the center). $(x - h)^2 + (y - k)^2 = r^2$		
Circumference	The distance around a circle; similar to the perimeter of a polygon. $C = \pi d$ or 2 pi R		
Clockwise	Moving in the direction of a clock.		
Coefficient	The numerical part of a term		
Collinear	Lying on the same line.		
Combinations	Different ways you can group elements in a set.		
Common Factors	Factors that two numbers have in common.		
Commutative Property of Multiplication	Property that states if x and y are two real numbers, then $x \times y = y \times x$.		
Complementary Angle	Adds up to a 90 degree angle.		
Complex Fractions	Fractions that contain more than one fraction line.		
Composite Functions	A combination of two functions, where you apply the first function and get an answer, and then fill *that answer* into the second function.		
Congruent	Identical in shape or measurement.		
Conjunction	A statement of two conditions, of which both must be true in order for the statement to be true.		
Conjugate	A binomials of the form $a + b_c$ and $a - b_c$.		
Consecutive Integers	Two integers whose difference is one.		
Constant	A quantity whose value is known and does not change.		
Conversion	Writing a given quantity using two different units of measurements.		

Math Terminology	Definition/Properties	Make an Example	Know It √
Coordinate Plane	A plane with a coordinate system that can be used to designate the position of any point on the plane.		
Corresponding Angles	Angles formed by two lines crossed by a transversal.		
Cross-Multiply	To set the cross products of a proportion equally. $\frac{a}{b} = \frac{c}{d} \rightarrow ad = cb$		
Cube	1) A regular solid having six congruent square faces. 2) To raise a number to the third power.		
Cube Root	A number, cubed, that gives an original number.		
Cylinder	An object shaped like a tube; a shape with straight sides and circular ends of equal size.		
Decimal	A number that's written in decimal form.		
Decrease from x to y	$x - y$		
Degree of Polynomial	The degree of the term in the polynomial that has the highest degree (the sum of the exponents of all the variables in that term).		
Degree	The unit measurement for angles > 45 degrees ⊢ 90 degrees — 180 degrees		
Denominator	The bottom number of a fraction.		
Dependent Probability	Probability questions with more than one scenario.		
Dependent Variable	In a function, the variable whose value depends on the value assigned to another variable.		
Determinant	One real number associated with a square matrix.		
Diagonal	A segment that extends from one vertex of a polygon to a vertex that's non-adjacent.		

Math Terminology	Definition/Properties	Make an Example	Know It √
Diameter	The distance from one edge to another on a circle through the centerpoint; it can be broken into two opposite radii so the length is equal to twice the circle's radius.		
Difference	The result of subtracting one number or quantity from another number or quantity.		
Digit	An integer between 0 and 9.		
Dimension	The number of spatial directions needed to create a geometric figure.		
Direct Variation	A linear function described by $y = m - x$, where $m \neq 0$.		
Directly Proportional	When increasing one quantity results in the increase of the other quantity (vary directly).		
Discriminate	The value of $b^2 - 4ac$ from $ax^2 + bx + c = 0$.		
Disjunction	A statement of two conditions in which only one condition must be true in order for the statement to be true.		
Distance	The length of the shortest path between two geometric objects.		
Distance Formula	For two points on a plane with coordinates (x, y) and (x^2, y^2) is d = $\sqrt{(x^2 - x)^2 + (y^2 - y)^2}$		
Distinct	Not equal.		
Distribute (Properties)	Multiply term by the variable in front of the parentheses. $a(b + c) = a \times b + a \times c$		
Dividend	A number or quantity that is divided by another number or quantity.		
Divisible	Divided evenly by a certain number with zero left over.		
Division	An inverse operation of multiplication.		
Divisor	A quantity which divides into another quantity.		
Domain	A set of all first coordinates of the ordered pairs of a relation.		

Math Terminology	Definition/Properties	Make an Example	Know It √
Domain of a Function	The complete set of possible values of the independent variable in the function/ the set of all possible x values which will make the function "work" and will output real *y*-values.		
Elements	Objects or numbers within a set.		
Eliminate Method	To eliminate one variable by adding equations.		
Ellipse $\frac{(x-h)^2}{a^2} + \frac{(y-k)^2}{b^2} = 1$	A set of all points so that the sum of the distances from two given points (called *foci*) is constant.		
Empty Set	A set that had no members, denoted by {}; also called a *null set ø*.		
Endpoints	Points in which all other points lie on the line segment.		
Equality	The property of two things being equal and symbolized by the equal sign (=).		
Equation	Quantities that are both equal.		
Equation of a line	Find the slope and y-intercept. Then the equation of the line can be written in slope-intercept form; y = mx + b.		
Equiangular Polygon	A polygon with all congruent angles.		
Equilateral Polygon	A polygon with all equal sides.		
Equilateral Triangle	A triangle with three equal angles that measure 60 degrees each and also equal side lengths.		
Equivalence	Stating that two quantities are equal in value.		
Evaluate	To replace variables of an expression with constants and then simplify them.		
Evaluate a Function	Insert a given *x* value, a number in the domain to see the result, which is a number in a range.		
Even Integer	An integer that's divisible by two with no remainder.		
Event	In statistics, the outcome of an experiment.		

Math Terminology	Definition/Properties	Make an Example	Know It √
Exclusive (numbers)	When either of two statements are true, but NOT BOTH.		
Expand	Using multiplication to eliminate the parentheses with an expression.		
Exponent	A shorthand notation used to indicate the number or value when a number is multiplied by itself a certain number of times (can be positive or negative). E.g., $3 \times 3 \times 3 \times 3 \times 3 = 3^5$ For positive exponents, multiply the base by itself. For negative exponents, take reciprocal of the positive. For several exponents with identical bases, multiply by adding exponents and divide by subtracting them. Raise exponential expressions by multiplying them and raising any number to exponent zero will equal one.		
Exponential Function	A function of form $y = b^2$ where k and b are constants and $b \neq 0$ or $b \neq 1$.		
Exponential Term	A quantity that contains exponents.		
Algebraic Expression	A quantity represented by variables and constants /or numbers.		
Exterior Angle Theorem	States that the exterior angle of a triangle is equal to the sum of the two remote interior angles.		
Face	A two-dimensional planar surface that makes part of a three-dimensional figure.		
Factor	A quantity that is a divisor of a larger number quantity without any remainders when the positive integers are multiplied by each to achieve the number. E.g., 8 has the factors of 2 & 4 ($2 \times 4 = 8$). It also has the factors of 8 & 1 ($8 \times 1 = 8$).		
Factorial	If n is an integer greater than zero , the factorial of a positive integer n, denoted by $n!$, is the product of all positive integers less than or equal to n.		

Math Terminology	Definition/Properties	Make an Example	Know It √
Factoring Algebraic Expressions	This involves breaking the expression down into two new expressions that when multiplied together give the original expression.		
FOIL	(First, Outer, Inner, Last). Used to multiply two algebra expressions. Multiply the First terms in each expression. Second, multiply the Outer expressions in the equation. Next, multiply the Inner terms. Lastly, multiply the Last terms.		
Formula	A mathematical sentence about relationships among certain quantities;		
Fraction	A ratio indicating the division of two quantities. (**Multiply** them by numerator times numerator and denominator times denominator. **Divide** them by multiplying one fraction by the reciprocal of the other one.)		
Functional Notation	The use of letters and parentheses to indicate a functional relationship, such as $f(x) = 2x^2 + 3$.		
Geometric Notations	AB means the distance from A to B. AB ←→ this line goes through both points A and B (arrows indicate infinity). AB —— line segments w/ endpoints A and B. AB —→ ray w/endpoint A thru B and infinity. BA —→ ray w/endpoint B thru A and infinity. ∠ABC the angle B is the vertex and A and C points on each ray. $m \angle B$ is the measure of angle B. △ABC is a triangle with A, B, C as vertices. □ABCD quadrilateral with A,B, C, D as vertices. AB ⊥ BC line segments AB and BC are perpendicular.		
Geometric Sequence $a_n = a^1 \times r^{n-1}$	Each term after the first is formed by multiplying the previous term by same factor.		

Math Terminology	Definition/Properties	Make an Example	Know It √
Graph Direction	**Negative** correlation; **Positive** correlation.		
Graph Transformation 1.) Basic function 2.) $y = x^3 + 5$ 3.) $y = x^3 - 5$ 4.) $y = (x + 5)^3$ 5.) $y = (x - 5)^3$ 6.) $y = (-x)^3$ 7.) $y = -x^3$	$y + x$ graph shifted *up* five units graph shifted *down* five units graph shifted *left* five units graph shifted *right* five units graph reflected over *y-axis* graph reflected over *x-axis*		
Graph	The mark(s) made on a coordinate plane that indicate the location of a point or set of points.		
Greater Than	$>$		
Great Than or Equal To	$\geq$		
Greatest Common Factor (GFC)	The product of all prime factors common in every two or more items.		
Height	One dimension of a geometric figure.		
Hence	"From now"—e.g., "How old will Leah be 4 years hence?"		
Hexagon	A polygon with six sides and six vertices; to measure the sum of the angles—(6 – 2) x 180, which totals a sum of 720°.		
Horizontal Distance	Distance measured only in the horizontal direction.		
Horizontal	A line on the xy plane that has zero slope.		
Hyperbola $\dfrac{(x-h)^2}{a^2} - \dfrac{(y-k)^2}{b^2} = 1$	The set of all points on a plane where the absolute value of the difference of the distances from two given points (foci) is constant.		
Hypotenuse	The side opposite the 90 degree angle in a right triangle (always the longest side in the triangle).		
Identity Function	A linear function such that $y = x$ or $f(x) = x$.		
Improper Fraction	A fraction with a numerator larger than the denominator.		

Math Terminology	Definition/Properties	Make an Example	Know It √
Inclusive	Includes the first and last elements.		
Inconsistent Equations	Equations with no common solution (like parallel lines).		
Increase from x to y	$y - x$		
Independent Events	In statistics, where the outcome of one event doesn't affect the probability of the occurrence of another event.		
Independent Probability	Separate probability questions that do not affect each other.		
Independent Variable	In a function, the variable whose value can be chosen.		
Index	The little number above and to the left of the radical sign that designates the root.		
Inequalities	Two values are not equal.		
Inequality	The relationship between two expressions that states that one expression is greater than the other.		
Input	The value plugged into a function to yield an output.		
Inscribed Angle	An angle with its vertex "on" the circle, formed by two intersecting chords.		
Integer	Any number that can be expressed without a symbol, fraction bar or decimal point (whole number). An integer can be zero, odd or even. **Even**—divided by 2 and no remainder. **Odd**—divided by 2 with remainder of 1. Any integer can be written over a 1.		
Integral	Referring to a number that's an integer.		
Intercept	The point where a line touches one of the coordinate axes on an xy plane.		
Interior Angle	The angle inside a polygon.		
Interior	A region that's enclosed by two or more geometric figures.		
Intersect	Having elements or points in common.		
Intersecting Lines	Where two lines meet.		

Math Terminology	Definition/Properties	Make an Example	Know It √
Intersection	Points that are common to two or more sets in a geometric figure.		
Intersection of Sets	When two or more sets have the same elements in common.		
Inverse Function [fog] (x) = [gof] (x) = x	Two polynomial functions, f and g, are inverse functions if and only if their compositions are identity functions.		
Inversely Proportional	When increasing one quantity decreases the other member-objects in a set.		
Inverse Variation	A relationship between two variables so that their product is constant.		
Irrational Number	A real number that can't be written as the ratio of two integers.		
Irregular	A geometric region that can't be described in a normal way.		
Is, as, was, has, cost	= (equals)		
Isosceles Triangle	A triangle with two congruent (equal) sides and two congruent angles		
Isosceles Right Triangle	Having one right angle and two congruent legs. $x : x : \sqrt{2}x$ proportion		
It's divisible by 2 if...	It's an even number.		
It's divisible by 3 if...	The digits add up to a multiple of three. E.g., (**195**) 1 + 9 + 5 = 15		
It's divisible by 4 if...	The last two digits **form** a number divisible by 4. E.g., 6,316,**832** (32 ÷ 4 = 8)		
It's divisible by 5 if...	It ends in a **5** or a **0**.		
It's divisible by 6 if...	It's divisible by 2 *and* 3. E.g., (**552**)		
It's divisible by 8 if...	The last three digits form a multiple of 8. E.g., (46,**352**) 352 ÷ 8 = 44		
It's divisible by 9 if...	Its digits add up to a multiple of 9. E.g., (**78,5214**) 7 + 8 + 5 + 2 + 1 + 4 = **27** (9 × 3 = 27)		
It's divisible by 10 if...	It ends in **0**. E.g., (**6490**)		

Math Terminology	Definition/Properties	Make an Example	Know It √
Lead Coefficient	In a polynomial, the co-efficient of the term with the greatest exponent.		
Least Common Multiple	The smallest quantity that two numbers can be divided evenly.		
Leg	One of two smaller sides of a right triangle, but not the hypotenuse.		
Length	The distance from the endpoint of a segment to the other.		
Less Than (symbol)	<		
Less Than (word problem)	To the left on the real number line.		
Less Than or Equal To	≤		
Like Terms	Monomials that differ from one another by their coefficients.		
Line	A geometric figure of two points and the union of all segments that contain the two points.		
Line Segments	A geometric figure of two endpoints and all the other points in between them.		
Line Formula	$y = mx + b$ (line has slope of m and a y-intercept of b). You can figure out the y-coordinate by multiplying the slope by the point's x-coordinate and then adding in the y-intercept.		
Linear Pair of Angles	Two angles that share a common side and whose unshared sides are collinear.		
Linear Equation	$ax + by + c = 0$, a first degree polynomial equation in one of more variables.		
Linear Function	$f(x) = mx + b$ where m and b are real numbers; to plot a point on a graph using (x, y), take x and separate it horizontally with the origin (0,0) and vertically separate y from points (x, y) and (0,0).		
Maximum	The largest possible quantity that satisfies a given set of conditions.		
Mean	The average of set of values.		

Math Terminology	Definition/Properties	Make an Example	Know It √
Median	Numbers ordered least to most with the middle exact number in an uneven set; if the set has an even amount of numbers, average the two numbers in the set that lie exactly in the middle.		
Midpoint	The point that's equidistant from both endpoints.		
Minimum	The smallest possible quantity that satisfies a given set of expressions.		
Mixed Numbers	A number that contains both an integer and a fraction.		
Mode	The elements/numbers that appear most often in a set.		
Monomial	A polynomial of one term.		
More (25 % **more**)	As many as, <u>plus</u> 25 % more.		
More Than	The number to the right of the real number line.		
Multi Variable Equation	An equation that contains more than one variable.		
Multiples	All numbers formed by the product of an integer and a given number. E.g., the multiples of 3 are 3, 6, 9, 12, 15, 18, 21, 24, 27…		
Multiplicative Inverse	For any number a if $a \neq 0$, $$a \times \frac{1}{a} = 1$$		
Multiplicative Identity	1 since $1 \times a = a$		
Multiplicative Property of Zero	Zero times any number is zero.		
n percent less than x	$x - (n/100)\ x$		
n percent greater than x	$x + (n/100)\ x$		
Natural Numbers	A set of numbers used to count things; also called *positive integers*.		

Math Terminology	Definition/Properties	Make an Example	Know It √
Negative	A quantity being less than zero.		
Negative Number	Is less than zero.		
Nested Functions	Functions within functions. The result returned from one function is used as the argument to another function.		
Non-Positive Number	Any negative number or zero.		
Nonzero Number	Any number besides zero.		
Null Set	The set that has no members, denoted by the notation ø.		
Numbers (Digits) Properties	**Places**: ones, tens, hundreds… **Distinct**: different, not identical **Consecutive**: in a row		
Number Sets	Putting numbers in specified position.		
Number Line	A line of infinite length with a center of 0 with positive and negative numbers (used to map entire set of real umbers).		
Numerator	The dividend within a fraction.		
Obtuse Angle	Angles that measure more than 90 degrees and less than 180 degrees.		
Odd	An integer that's not evenly divided by two.		
Odds	The successful outcome of an event expressed as the ratio of the number of ways it can succeed to the number of ways it can fail.		
Of	Multiplied by		
Opposite	The side opposite of the angle or side.		
Opposite Numbers	The same distance from zero on a number line, only in the other direction.		
Order of Operations PEMDAS	The order in which operations are performed on an algebraic expression. "**P**lease **E**xcuse **M**y **D**ear **A**unt **S**ally"— Parentheses, Exponents, Multiply, Divide, Add, Subtract.		

Math Terminology	Definition/Properties	Make an Example	Know It √
Ordered Pair	Numbers used to specify the position of a point on the xy-plane.		
Origin	A point on xy-plane whose coordinates are (0,0).		
Outcome	A possible result in a probability problem.		
Parabola	The set of all points which in a plane are equally distant from a given point and a given line not containing the point (quadratic graph).		
Parallel	Two lines with the same slope that lie on the same plane.		
Parallelogram	Its opposite sides are parallel, and it has two pairs of equal angles and four pairs of supplementary angles. All angles = 360°.		
Pattern	A repeated ordering of numbers or values.		
Pentagon	A special polygon with five sides. The sum of the angles = 540°.		
Percent	The percent number expressed as a fraction with 100 as the denominator (number of parts per hundred—take the proportion and divide the numerator by the denominator and multiply it by 100).		
Percentage	One number is compared to 100 by Direct Proportion; increasing both proportions equally.		
Percent Decrease	The amount of decrease divided by the original amount.		
Percent Increase from x to y ($y > x$)	$(y - x / x)\ 100$		
Percent Increase	The amount of increase divided by the original amount.		
Perfect Cube	An integer that's equal to another integer raised to the third power.		
Perfect Square	An integer that's equal to another integer raised to the second power.		

Math Terminology	Definition/Properties	Make an Example	Know It √
Perimeter	Measurement of the shapes outside border by adding all the sides.		
Permutation	Arranging things in a certain order; the "counting method," where if a choice can be made in a ways and a second choice can be made in b ways, then $a \times b$ will be the answer.		
Perpendicular	Two lines intersect and form a right angle.		
Place Value	Referring to the value of a digit in the base-10 number system.		
Pi ($\pi \approx 3.14$)	The ratio of the circumference to the diameter of that circle.		
Pie Chart	A circular chart divided into sectors, illustrating percents. The arc length of each sector (its central angle and area) is proportional to the quantity it represents, and the sectors create a full disk.		
Pictograph	A way of representing statistical data using symbolic figures to match the frequencies of different kinds of data.		
Plane	A set of points spanned by two intersecting lines and all the points between them.		
Plotting Points	A rectangular coordinate system where a set of two intersecting and perpendicular axes form an xy plane. The horizontal axis is labeled the x axis, and the vertical axis is labeled the y axis. They divide the plane into four parts called *quadrants*. Any point on the plane corresponds to an ordered pair (x,y) of real numbers x and y. x is called the x-coordinate and y is called the y-coordinate.		
Point (x,y)	The geometric figure formed at the intersection of two distinct lines.		

Math Terminology	Definition/Properties	Make an Example	Know It √
Polygon	A closed figure in a plane having three or more sides. To measure the sum of the angles, subtract 2 from the number of sides and multiply by 180. To find the perimeter, add all the lengths of the sides. To find the area (not a triangle or parallelogram), divide it into smaller polygons and proceed to find the area for each polygon.		
Polynomial	One term or a sum of individual terms, each having the form ax.		
Positive Number	A number greater than zero.		
Preceding	Coming immediately before.		
Prime Number	A positive integer whose factors are one and the number itself. It's always positive; 2 is the only even prime number; 1 is not prime because it has only 1 factor.		
Prime Number Ratio	Relationship is expressed with a colon between the numbers. E.g., 3:1.		
Prime Factors	Factors that are prime numbers.		
Probability/Chance	Probability = ratio of number of desired outcomes and total number of outcomes in the sample space. Chance = number of times a certain thing could happen or number of times any of the things could happen.		
Product	The result of multiplying two or more numbers/quantities together.		
Profit	The difference between income and expenses.		
Proportion	Equality between two ratios (written as a fraction 4/3).		
Pythagorean Theorem $a^2 + b^2 = c^2$	Adding the squares of the two legs of a right triangle will add to equal the square of the hypotenuse		

Math Terminology	Definition/Properties	Make an Example	Know It √
Pythagorean Theorem 3D	The same triangle facing a different way, but 3D! If we call the sides x, y and z instead of a, b and d, we get: $x^2 + y^2 + z^2 = distance^2$ Measure the x-coordinate [left/right distance], the y-coordinate [front/back distance], and the z-coordinate [up/down distance]. And now we can find the 3D distance to a point given its coordinates!		
Pythagorean Triple Special Right Triangles	Consists of three numbers that can all be the lengths of the sides of a right triangle. Example: {3, 4, 5} is the same as $3^2 + 4^2 = 5^2$ {1, 1, $\sqrt{2}$} is the same as $1^2 + 1^2 = \sqrt{2}^2$ {1, $\sqrt{3}$, 2} is the same as $1^2 + \sqrt{3}^2 = 2^2$ {5, 12, 13} is the same as $5^2 + 12^2 = 13^2$ To get another Pythagorean triple, multiply the same number by each side. E.g., {9, 12, 15} is simply {3, 4, 5} multiplied by 3.		
Quadrant	One of the four regions in the xy-plane that form the xy-axis.		
Quadratic Equation	It involves three terms. In an equation in the form of $a^x + b^x + c = 0$, one unknown has the number 2 as the highest power of the variable; one term is a variable not raised to any power; one term is a regular number with no variable. E.g., $x^2 + 5^x = 20$; solved by factoring.		
Quadratic Formula $x = \dfrac{-b \pm \sqrt{b^2 - 4ac}}{2a}$	That **amazing** formula for finding all values of x that satisfy the equation $ax^2 + bx + c = 0$. Works even if you can't factor the left-hand side.		
Quadrilateral	A four-sided polygon with four angles. The five most common types are parallelogram, rectangle, square, trapezoid and rhombus.		
Quarter Circle	Part of a circle that is one-fourth the area of a circle.		

Math Terminology	Definition/Properties	Make an Example	Know It √
Quotient	The number of times a divisor will completely divide into a given quantity.		
Radical Expression	An expression that involves a root.		
Radical Sign	A symbol denoting a root.		
Radicand	A number underneath the radical sign.		
Radius	A segment extending from the edge point on the perimeter of a circle to the center of the circle. The radii of a circle have the same length.		
Remainders	The number left over when you divide one number by another and it doesn't come out even.		
Range (of function)	Set of numbers that $f(x)$ which come out equal. E.g., $f(x) = x^3 + 6$ has range of both negative and positive infinity. The function $f(x) = \sqrt{x}$ only has range of non-negative numbers.		
Range	The difference between the greatest and least values in a set of data.		
Rate	Distance or jobs divided by time, or price per item.		
Ratio	The comparison of two numbers expressed by dividing one by the other (another name for a *fraction*). E.g., 3:1.		
Ratio of Sides	Right Triangle: determined by comparing the lengths of two sides (opposite side divided by adjacent side).		
Rational Number	Any number that can be written as the quotient of integers (division by zero excluded).		
Rational Expression	An algebraic expression written in the form of a fraction.		
Rational Equation	An equation containing one or more rational expressions.		
Rationalizing	The process of eliminating radicals from the denominators.		

Math Terminology	Definition/Properties	Make an Example	Know It √
Real Number	Any number that can be found on the number line.		
Reciprocal	The product of a number and its reciprocal is always one (opposite number where numerator and denominator swap places).		
Rectangle	A four-sided figure with four interior right angles—they are parallelograms with all angles measuring 90°.		
Rectangular Box or Solid	A three-dimensional object with six sides, all of which are rectangles.		
Reflection Line	A line that acts as a mirror in the form of a perpendicular bisector so that corresponding points are the same distance from the mirror.		
Reflexive Property	For any number a, $a = a$.		
Regular Polygon	A closed geometric figure with at least three sides, where the interior angles and sides are congruent.		
Relation	A set of ordered pairs.		
Remainder	The fractional part that remains after dividing.		
Respectively	In the same order; e.g., Dustin, Derek and Drake are 5, 3, and 2, respectively.		
Right Triangle	A triangle with one interior angle measuring 90°.		
Rise	A vertical change from any one point to another.		
Run	A horizontal change from any one point to another.		
Scalene Triangle	A triangle that has no sides of equal length.		
Scatter Plot	A diagram using Cartesian coordinates to display values for two variables for a set of data. It's displayed as a collection of points, each having the value of one variable determining the position on the horizontal axis and the value of the other variable determining the position on the vertical axis.		

Math Terminology	Definition/Properties	Make an Example	Know It √
Scientific Notations	A number in the form of $a \times 10^n$, where $1 \leq a < 10$, and n is an integer.		
Second Degree Equation	Any equation with terms having 2 as its highest exponent.		
Sector	A region of a circle bounded by an arc and a central angle.		
Segment	A line segment.		
Semicircle	Half a circle.		
Sequence	A set of numbers in a specified order; they can stop at a point or go on to infinity. Some sequences follow a pattern of addition or multiplication.		
Set	A collection of numbers or objects; things in a set are called members or elements.		
Set Notation	A method of designing a set by enclosing the numbers of the set within brackets.		
Side	A segment that makes up one part of a figure in a plane.		
Similar Triangle Rule	The smaller triangle is similar to the larger triangle if the bases are parallel: their relationship is the same between any two corresponding sides.		
Similar	Having the same shape but not the same size.		
Simplifying	Adding, subtracting, multiplying and dividing in an expression by combining like terms.		
Slope	The ratio of the rise to the run between two points on the line. (Intercept form : $y = mx + b$)		
Solids	A geometric figure having three dimensions.		
Square	1) The result when a number is multiplied by itself. 2) A rectangle which has four equal sides.		
Square Root	A number that when squared, yields x. $(\sqrt{x})^2 = x$		

Math Terminology	Definition/Properties	Make an Example	Know It √
Squared Quantity	A quantity within an expression which is raised to the second power.		
Standard Form	A linear equation in the form of $ax + by = c$ where a, b and c are real and a and b are not both zero.		
Straight Angle	An angle that measures 180° (straight line).		
Subscripted Variable	A variable with a subscript—a little letter slightly below and to the right of the variable.		
Substitution	Expressing a variable, expression or constant having the same value.		
Successive	Directly following.		
Sum	The result of addition.		
Supplementary Angles	Two angles that measure 180°.		
Surface Area	The total area of all the faces or surfaces of a three-dimensional figure.		
Surface Area of Cube	$6l^2$, where l = the length of side.		
Surface Area of Prism	Rectangle: 2(wh + lw + lh) Triangle: 2(Area of the base) + (Perimeter of the base) (Altitude)		
Synthetic Division	A shortcut method used to divide polynomials by binomials.		
System	A collection of two or more equations or inequalities.		
Systems of Equations and Inequalities	Two or more mathematical statements considered at the same time.		
Tangent to a Circle	A line that touches the circle at one point; a tangent line is perpendicular to the radius at the point shared by the tangent and the circle.		
Tenths	The first decimal place to the right of the decimal point.		
Term	A number and/or one or more variables multiplied together.		
Thousandths	The third decimal place to the right of the decimal point.		

Math Terminology	Definition/Properties	Make an Example	Know It √
Time	A variable related to distance and time by the equation. rate • time = distance		
Transitive Property	For all numbers a, b and c, if a = b and b = c then a = c.		
Translation of Function	A graph of a function can be moved up, down, left or right by adding (moves it up) or subtracting (moves it down) from the output or the input.		
Transposition	Changing sides and changing signs.		
Transversal Line	A line that cuts across two or more (usually parallel) lines.		
Trapezoid	A quadrilateral with one pair of parallel sides.		
Triangle	A three-sided polygon (The sum of the angles are the same as a straight line—180 degrees. Longest side opposite biggest angle/Shortest side opposite smallest angle.) **The length of each side must be less than the length of the total sum of the other two sides**. (If not, the triangle could not "close.")		
Triangular Inequality Theorem	The sum of any two sides of a triangle that is greater than the third side.		
Trinomial	A polynomial of three terms.		
Union	A set consisting of all members of set A and set B.		
Unit's Digit	The number that's farthest to the right or the first digit to the left of the decimal point. E.g., in 34,672, the unit's or one's digit is "2."		
Value (Fair Market)	The amount of goods considered to be fair for something else.		
Variable	A quantity represented by a letter whose value may vary.		

Math Terminology	Definition/Properties	Make an Example	Know It √
Venn Diagram	Made up of two or more overlapping circles. It's often used in mathematics to show all hypothetically possible logical relations between a finite collection of sets.		
Vertex Angle	The angle formed by the two sides in an isosceles triangle. The angle located opposite the base is called the vertex.		
Vertex	The point where two sides of an angle or polygon intersect.		
Vertical	The direction of the y-axis.		
Vertical Distant	The distance between two points on the xy-plane represented by the change in the y-coordinates.		
Vertical Line Test	A test use to determine if a relation is a function. A relation is a function if there are no vertical lines that intersect the graph at more than one point.		
Vertical Angles	Non-adjacent angles formed by two intersecting lines.		
Volume	The measurement of how much space a figure takes up.		
Volume of Cube	Cube the length of an edge of the cube.		
Volume of Prism	The area of the base times the altitude.		
Whole Number	A non-negative number that has no fractional or decimal part.		
Width	One of the measurements used to calculate the area of a rectangle, or the volume of a rectangular box.		
x older than y	$x + y$		
x younger than y	$y - x$		
x and y	$x + y$		
x-coordinate	One of the coordinates to specify a point on the xy-axis.		
y years from now	$+ y$		
y years ago	$- y$		

Math Terminology	Definition/Properties	Make an Example	Know It √
y-coordinate	One of the coordinates to specify a point on the xy-axis.		
Zero Product Property	For any numbers a and b, if $ab = 0$ then $a = 0$ and $b = 0$.		
Zero Exponent	$x^0 = 1$ where $x \neq 0$		

APPENDIX C:

My Motivation Test

MY MOTIVATION TEST

AS HUMAN BEINGS, WE are all motivated by something, but we are not all motivated by the same thing(s). It is important to figure out what will be the catalyst that will help you to make studying for the SAT and PSAT a priority. Below is a fun quiz for you to fill out. It is simply used as a guideline to help you set some test prep goals that you can readily achieve by finding out what motivates you.

Read each line below and pick the one that best suits you. If you find that both descriptions apply, pick the one statement that has been more dominate in your life in the past.

Next, score your answers. Use the first letter of each section to create your motivational trait. Next find the title that bests depicts your motivational style.

Finally, using the suggested questions, create a game plan that will help you chart your course to stay on track and reach your test score goals.

As human beings, we are all motivated by something, but we are not all motivated by the same thing(s).

MY MOTIVATIONAL TRAIT

Circle the letter that best represents you:

I am a loyal person and I have a few intimate friends.	A
I strive for goals and want to reach the top by surpassing others.	B
Others may see me as insecure at times.	A
My confidence can sometimes overwhelm others.	B
I usually like being the leader.	A
Usually I prefer others to take the lead.	B
For the most part, I am congenial and very laid-back.	A
For the most part, I am intensely ambitious, positive and self-assured.	B
I am a planner.	A
I just let things happen.	B
Basically, I'd rather conform and fit in.	A
Basically, I'd rather stand out from the crowd.	B
I like to pacify people and keep the status quo.	A
It's a test to me to question the existing state of affairs.	B

TOTAL

A	B

Count the number of A's and B's. Which column is higher?
If A is higher, you are a Supervisor.(S)
If B is higher, you are an Associate. (A)

Write your title_____ Write first letter of title_____

I can be bold and impulsive.	C
I like to analyze and calculate the situation.	D
I enjoy being rewarded for my accomplishments.	C
I make contributions that are significant to me.	D
I am invigorated and determined and I like to be stimulated.	C
I seek to keep the peace and maintain a steady pace in my life.	D
I am constantly thinking of new and exciting ideas and I love to include others in the process.	C
Follow-through and making sure the job is done right is very important to me.	D
I like to be innovative and deal with problems on the spur of the moment.	C
Being attentive and planning for the future is a major strength of mine.	D
I lean toward spontaneity and risk-taking.	C
I lean toward being orderly, concentrated, and disciplined.	D
Details bore me and I don't like them.	C
I like dealing with details.	D

I thrive on challenges and discovering new things first-hand. C
I like to keep the peace and maintain a stable environment. D

Changer (C)
Balancer (D)

TOTAL

C	D

Count the number of C's and D's. Which column is higher?
If C is higher, you are a Changer. (C)
If D is higher, you are a Balancer (D)

Write your title_____ Write first letter of title____

Personal recognition and financial success are important to me. E
Making an important difference means more to me than financial gain. F

I like it when I am recognized publicly. E
I would prefer to be recognized privately. F

Obtaining material possessions is very important to me. E
Obtaining material possessions in not very important to me. F

Gaining my own fortune is more important to me. E
I want to be known for my legacy of contribution to the world. F

I am mainly interested in salary and benefits when it comes to
looking for a job.   E

I desire to hold a job that gives me personal pleasure
more than the pay and perks.   F

I am a people-pleaser and am concerned of what others think of me.   E

I don't care what people think of me.   F

Outside (E)
Inside (F)

TOTAL

E	F

Count the number of E's and F's. Which column is higher?

If E is higher, your motivation comes from Outside. (O)

If F is higher, your motivation comes from Inside.(I)

Write your title_____ Write first letter of title_____

Take the first letter of each title/trait and write it here: __ __ __

Now match up the motivational trait below.

(SBI) MANAGER

Managers tend to be:

- Very responsible
- Detailed problem-solvers
- Organized and structured
- Practical
- Positive contributors
- Strategic thinker
- Time-managers
- Goal-oriented

Create a test prep plan that maintains consistency and accountability with clear goals that are outlined for success. Track your progress daily with a steady routine using charts and spreadsheets. Mark your calendar with specific goals for improvement. Start a competition that makes the reward benefit yourself as well as others when you have reached your goal. (ex. When you reach a goal, have others pledge money to give to your favorite charity or help others who are less fortunate with their prep goals.)

Checklist for Reaching Test Score Goals:

☐ What is my test prep goal?_____

☐ Make a <u>daily</u> spreadsheet/chart with specific goals

☐ Mark calendar with goal deadlines

☐ Accountability Partner_____

☐ Start a competition

How will it benefit me?_____

How will it benefit others?_____

☐ Like-minded friends to team up with:

_____

_____

_____

_____

_____

☐ My reward for reaching my goal(s)_____

(SCI) DREAMER

Dreamers tend to be:

- Visionary
- Confident
- Multi-tasker
- Creative
- Imaginative
- Energetic
- Original Thinker
- Innovator
- Persistent

Create an inspiring practice time with original ideas for achieving test prep goals. Make a list of several ways to accomplish how you can reach higher scores. Make the goals enjoyable and exciting and change them up daily. Stick to only the ones that work for you. Make a detailed record of why this is important to you and review it daily. Write down the consequences if you don't reach your goal. How will this goal benefit you as well as others?

Checklist For Reaching Test Score Goals:

☐ What is my test prep goal?_____

☐ Make a list of ideas to reach goals (fun and exciting)

1. _____

2. _____

3. _____

4. _____

5. _____

☐ Why is this goal important to me?_____

☐ Consequences of not reaching my goal._____

☐ How will this goal benefit me?_____
_____

☐ How will this goal benefit
others?_____

☐ Friends that can help lead me to success

_____

_____

_____

_____

☐ My reward for reaching my goal(s)_____

_____

_____

(SBO) LEADER

Leaders tend to be:

- Independent
- Determined
- Strong-minded
- Quick-decision makers
- Methodical
- Organized
- Planner

Create a consistent plan to work a little bit each day on my goals in small manageable pieces with a set deadline. Make sure the goals have a specific objective and there can be some public recognition for your accomplishments. Plan to reward yourself along the way each time a goal is reached. Make sure the reward is tangible and something that you really want.

Checklist for Reaching Test Score Goals:

☐ What is my test prep goal?_____

☐ Specific Daily Goals_____

Daily_____

Weekly_____

Monthly_____

Yearly_____

☐ Deadline to reach goal_____

☐ My Incremental Reward (for achievements toward my goal)

    Daily_____

    Weekly_____

    Monthly_____

    Yearly_____

(SCO) CHALLENGER

The Challenger tends to be:

- Charismatic
- Engaging
- Negotiators
- Risk-takers
- Popular
- Fun-loving
- Fighter
- Enthusiastic

Create a plan that fits into your busy schedule. It is imperative that you block off specific time to work on your goals and be flexible to make sure it gets done. Discipline yourself to be consistent and avoid busy-work. Start a challenging competition that ends with an equally rewarding prize. Find like-minded achievers to join in on the contest. Make sure the process is fun and enjoyable.

Checklist for Reaching Test Score Goals:

☐ What is my test prep goal?_____

☐ How can I make studying
enjoyable?_____

☐ How much time will I spend
daily?_____

☐ What time of day? (If I miss it, what are my back-up plans?)

     Plan A_____

     Plan B_____

     Plan C_____

☐ Start a competition._____

☐ Friends that I will involve in the competition:

     _____

     _____

     _____

     _____

     _____

     _____

☐ My reward for reaching my goal(s)_____

_____

(ABI) SUPERVISOR

Supervisors tend to be:

- Loyal
- Dependable
- Detail-oriented
- Methodical
- Caring
- Supportive
- Conscientious
- Practical

Create a realistic goal that can be achieved in a reasonable time frame. Don't be hard on yourself to be perfect. Find others who are as equally committed to test success. Use teamwork to work toward individual and team goals. Find a support group who will cheer you on along the way. Reward yourself by celebrating success privately with a few close people.

Checklist for Reaching Test Score Goals:

☐ What is my individual test prep goal?_____

☐ When can I expect to accomplish my goal?_____
_____

☐ Friends to team up with:

_____

_____

_____

_____

_____

_____

_____

_____

☐ What are my team test prep (score) goals?_____

☐ Resources I will use_____

☐ My support group_____

☐ My reward for reaching my goal(s)_____

(ACI) CONNECTOR

- Outgoing
- Friendly
- Creative
- Caring
- Resourceful
- Adventurous
- Loyal
- Dependable

Create a test prep plan that works together with a partner or a group of like-minded people trying to reach the same goal. Accountability is very important to make sure you follow-through with your plan. Work daily on your goal-even if it is a small amount because this will move you closer to your goal. Don't isolate yourself to try and do this on your own. Daily refer to why your goal is important to you.(Post it in clear site.)

☐ What is my test prep goal?_____

☐ Why is it important to me?_____

_____

(Look at the above reasons <u>each</u> day to remind you to do something every day to work toward your goal.)

☐ My partner or the group who I will work with:

        _____

        _____

        _____

        _____

☐ My support group for accountability_____

☐ My reward for reaching my goal(s)_____

_____

(ABO) POLISHER

- Disciplined
- Focused
- Systematic Thinker
- Conscientious

- Diligent
- Deliberate
- Dependable
- Analytical

Create the best possible way for you to reach your goal by researching the ideal way to achieve it. You may seek to be coached by a mentor. Research all the facts and find others who have already accomplished your dream and ask them for assistance. Make sure you set back a significant portion of money that you have allotted to splurge on yourself when you have met your desired goal each week.

Checklist for Reaching Test Score Goals:

☐ What is my test prep goal?_____

☐ What is the best way to reach my goal?_____

_____

☐ Who can mentor me?_____

☐ People I know who have achieved the same goal:

_____

_____

_____

_____

_____

_____

_____

☐ Money that I will set aside each week to splurge_____

_____

☐ My reward for reaching my goal(s)_____

_____

_____

(ACO) INVESTIGATOR

- Adventurous
- Considerate
- Thoughtful
- Insightful
- Perceptive
- Impulsive
- Energetic
- Creative

Create a goal that involves others that you can encourage along the way. Working together with others can help you stay excited about your goals as well as make the studying process fun. Make a list of all the ways that have helped others reach the same goal and work on all of them. Learn a new strategy each week. Reward yourself with something small at every stage and when you have completed your goal, give yourself a big reward.

Checklist for Reaching Test Score Goals:

☐ What is my test prep goal?_____

☐ What are some different ways to reach my goal?

_____

_____

_____

_____

_____

_____

☐ Who can I involve so that we can reach this common goal:

_____

_____

_____

_____

_____

☐ My reward for reaching my daily goal_____

_____

☐ My reward for reaching my weekly goal_____

_____

☐ My reward for reaching my monthly goal_____

_____

☐ My BIG reward for reaching my final goal_____

_____